Treasures in The Darkness

"And I will give you the treasures of darkness…"
Isaiah 45:3

The OMS Journey
in Hong Kong

by

Dorothy Backer

Backer, Dorothy
TREASURES IN THE DARKNES:
The OMS Journey in Hong Kong

ISBN 1-800338-36-X

Printed in the United States of America

DEDICATION

This is dedicated to my dear co-workers in the Hong Kong Evangelical Church, and especially to Rev. Simon Lee, who was my pastor for a few years until God took him at the age of 32. His great love and burden was for his "tung baau," his people of China, to hear and know about Jesus Christ.

~~~~

To these dear ones and to the many co-workers who went before, we give thanks, for they are the prime history makers in our OMS Hong Kong history.

~~~~

"I thank my God every time I remember you. In all my prayers for all of you, I always pray with joy because of your partnership in the gospel from the first day until now, being confident of this, that He who began a good work in you will carry it on to completion until the day of Christ Jesus" **(Philippians 1:3-6).**

ACKNOWLEDGMENTS

Much of the material of this book has come from old prayer letters of Mrs. Florence Munroe and copies of quarterly reports from the early co-workers kept on file in the OMS office in Hong Kong. Bits and pieces came from early copies of the *Missionary Standard* and later the *OMS Outreach*. I have tried to give credit in the NOTES to those who wrote the articles used. My thanks go to the Hong Kong missionaries both present and past who have been so gracious to send e-mails to answer my questions and give facts and figures to my thoughts.

Rev. Grant Nealis, former OMS Hong Kong Field Director, helped me by reading what I wrote early on and giving me direction and suggestions. Dr. Ed Kilbourne, who wrote a big book for OMS' 100-year anniversary, has been a wonderful encourager. Rev. Buddy Gaines, a former OMS HK missionary, in his adventures around the world for OMS and Evangelism Explosion, sent me a message from Siberia. Now that is a miracle in itself. EE in Siberia? Yes!

Rev. Dave and Cindy Aufrance, present OMS HK Field Directors, sat down with me in the beginning and brainstormed ideas. They also did a tape of all that they could remember of OMS HK events, which was a terrific help. All along Dave and Cindy have encouraged me and urged me onward. Thanks so much!

To those of our Chinese leadership who gave me time for interviews, I send my gratitude for their time, testimonies, and friendship.

If you with better memories than I find some errors, please forgive my not-so-accurate recollections and enjoy the overview of how God has led OMS in Hong Kong these past 46 years.

"Auntie Mun" holding one of the refugee babies.

Charles Cowman

Ernest A. Kilbourne

Juji Nakada

Three men whose hearts were set on fire to reach men and women all across Japan for Jesus Christ, then to other nations of the world. In 1901 The Oriental Missionary Society (now OMS International) was begun in Tokyo, Japan.

CONTENTS

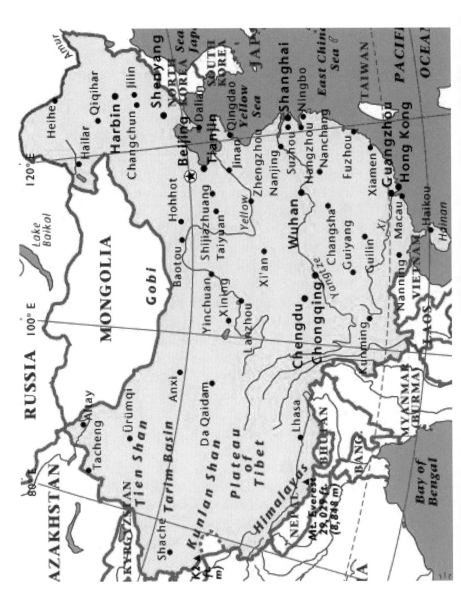

The map of China – Hong Kong isn't even a dot on the Southern coast of China between Hainan Island and Taiwan.

CHAPTER 1

BRIEF HISTORY OF HONG KONG

And men had to come from the Far West to give it a
name in the history of the East.

E. J. Eitel, *Europe in China,* 1895

A British colony situated on the southeast coast of China, Hong Kong is comprised of the island of that name obtained in 1841, the district of Kowloon on the mainland secured in 1860 along with Stonecutters Island, and a larger area of the mainland called the New Territories. This area was leased for 99 years in 1898 and covers 355 square miles. In the form of a peninsula with its northern boundary roughly along the Shum Chun River from Deep Bay to the northern shore of Mirs Bay, it includes 235 islands, the biggest being Lantau. The island of Hong Kong from which the colony takes its name is 32 square miles, less than one-tenth the size of the New Territories. Kowloon is only a tenth of the size of the island, being only three and a half square miles.

Hong Kong lies just within the tropics at the mouth of the Pearl River and has a monsoon type of climate. The monsoons dominated the navigation of the China Sea by the early western traders, and as long as ships carried sail, their influence was always important. Hong Kong also lies within the typhoon zone.

The climate with its high humidity, extremes of temperature, and threat of typhoons makes living uncomfortable for about half the year.

The Portuguese opened the sea routes in the 16th century and settled in Macau in 1557. The Spaniards, Dutch, English, and French followed, all seeking trade, lured by the fable of the riches of Cathay. During the 18th century the commerce between China and the West had largely passed into British hands. They were able to make products of India and the East Indies available, and the British had become a nation of tea-drinkers, making them China's best customers. Unfortunately, the conditions under which the trade was handled gave rise to much dissatisfaction, out of which the colony of Hong Kong eventually arose.[1]

The Opium Wars seemed to be the result of the intense desire of the British to have open ports in China with freedom to trade. The largest commodity that the English had was opium from India, and the Chinese took that in exchange for tea and silver. The Chinese emperor did not want the opium brought into China, leading to the enslavement of the people. Many misunderstandings arose between the English and the Chinese, as well as between the English government and those Englishmen who were stationed in the China area, mainly in Macau. Hong Kong was an island with a good harbor close enough to Canton. Captain Charles Elliot as the plenipotentiary in charge of the negotiations with China arranged to have the island of Hong Kong ceded to England as partial settlement of one of the wars. Hong Kong was occupied on January 26, 1841, by a naval force under Commodore Sir J. J. Gordon Bremer, Senior Naval Officer, which landed and raised the flag at Possession Point. Almost two and a half years elapsed before the British government recognized this as the birth of a new colony.

Lord Palmerston, the British Foreign Secretary, recalled Captain Elliot to England. He was not impressed by the cession of Hong Kong, "a barren island with hardly a house upon it." Palmerston did not believe that Hong Kong would become the mart of trade anymore than Macau had.[2]

At the time of the foreseen second Opium War, Lord Palmerston was Prime Minister. He was 75 years old when it erupted. Many of the English people deprecated the war with China over the sale of opium. Palmerston's son-in-law, Lord Ashley, had this to say: "We have triumphed in one of the most lawless, unnecessary, and unfair struggles in the records of history, this cruel and debasing war. The whole world is intoxicated with the prospect of Chinese trade. Altars to Mammon are rising on every side and thousands of cotton children will be sacrificed to his honor."

But when he read the terms of the treaty, he denounced them equally. The peace was as wicked as the war itself. For him, as for Wilberforce before him, to champion any moral cause was to fight for God. On March 23, 1843, he wrote, "Prayer to begin, prayer to accompany, and prayer to close any undertaking for His service is the secret of all prospering in our ways. Oh, what a question is this opium affair; bad as I thought it, I find it a thousand times worse, more black, more cruel, more Satanic than all the deeds of private sin in the records of prison history."

On April 4, 1843, he introduced the resolution in Parliament: "That it is the opinion of this House that the continuance of the trade in opium and the monopoly of its growth in … India are destructive of all relations of amity between England and China … and utterly inconsistent with the honor and duties of a Christian kingdom; and that steps be taken as soon as possible to abolish the evil."[3]

3

Numerous wars in China had their effects on the development of Hong Kong. In the early 1900s Japan began to have her eyes on China. Civil war within the country made it easier for Japan to gain a foothold. Dr. Sun Yat Sen died in 1925 and his successor, Chiang Kai-shek, took over. He established the National Government of the Republic of China controlled by the Kuomintang. The hostilities between Japan and China merged into the World War of 1939-1945. During that time many Chinese fled south and into Hong Kong. When Japan took over Hong Kong, Christmas of 1941, they were caught and for three years and eight months all people in Hong Kong suffered a harrowing occupation by the Japanese troops.[4]

Since the tenth century, Hong Kong had become the southernmost Chinese settlement and place of refuge for those who wanted to escape internal turmoil or foreign invasion on the China mainland. Whenever China quivered with political tremors or natural disasters, her people spilled into Hong Kong. In the 20th century these included the times of Japanese invasions, the civil war between the Nationalists and the Communists under Mao Tse Tung, then the Communist takeover of the country, famines in the late 1950s, and the Cultural Revolution of 1966-1976.

The Bamboo Curtain dropped in 1949 as Communist forces took over. No more communication was possible with the OMS workers left behind, and the OMS centers in Peking, Shanghai, Nanking, and Canton had closed their doors. Attention turned to the refugee-ridden British colony of Hong Kong. On the very doorstep of Communist China, Hong Kong, with millions of Chinese, still remained free and wide open to the Gospel. Refugees from the mainland flooded Hong Kong, living everywhere. Shacks sprouted like weeds on hillsides.

4

People were crammed together like sardines, taking every available space.

The "H" Blocks built during the 50's and 60's to house the many refugees. Some of the rooftops are fenced in and being used. Some have not been occupied.

Rev. Harry Woods, while in Hong Kong, baptized this group of new believers.

Rev. Harry Woods and Dr. Eugene Erny (fourth President of OMS) looking at relief map of Hong Kong.

CHAPTER 2

BEGINNINGS OF THE
ORIENTAL MISSIONARY SOCIETY

In 1901 God inspired two telegraph operators in Chicago, Charles E. Cowman and Ernest A. Kilbourne, together with their friend, Rev. Juji Nakada, to start evangelistic work in Tokyo, Japan. The mission was established under the name the Oriental Missionary Society. The work extended to Korea in 1907, China in 1925, and India in 1940, spreading to South America, Taiwan, Hong Kong, Spain, Indonesia, and recently Mozambique. In 1973 the name of the Oriental Missionary Society was changed to include the initials OMS and add International. This made it easier for countries not in the Orient to translate the name for their legal registrations and other official business. OMS International now serves in over 43 countries around the world.

HONG KONG BEGINNINGS

Massive gates often swing on the hinges of small circumstances. In this case the door of opportunity for our work in Hong Kong hinged on the guidance of God's Spirit to a widow, a former missionary to China. She began as a single missionary working in Hong Kong with the Peniel Mission. She met Rev. Eldridge Munroe after his wife had died. They were married in 1932 and worked with the South China Holiness Mission in Canton. This work was later combined with that of the Oriental

Missionary Society. In 1949 when the Communists took over China, many were forced to flee and the Munroes went back to the United States.

In February 1953 Mrs. Florence Munroe's missionary husband, the Rev. E. R. Munroe, passed away. Although nearing the age of retirement, she still felt the call of the Chinese people within her heart. Because of her deep commitment to God and her love for the Chinese, she told OMS leaders that she felt she should return to Hong Kong.

When she arrived on November 28, 1953, the OMS directors in the Orient, Rev. E. L. Kilbourne and Rev. Harry F. Woods, met with her in Hong Kong to make plans and counsel together concerning the future work in the area.

As OMS had never worked in Hong Kong, Mrs. Munroe wondered where to begin. She began looking for some of the OMS workers and students she knew that had come from the OMS seminary in Canton, China. She heard that Mr. Ho Yui Chi was in Macau and sent him a telegram to come to Hong Kong. They located several others who came to help for a while.

In December 1953 Mrs. Munroe found an empty hall located in Sham Shui Po district. This was one of God's miracles because suitable places were expensive and people were everywhere. On Christmas night a tragic fire swept through Shek Kip Mei Valley, destroying acres of shacks and leaving 60,000 squatters homeless. When Mrs. Munroe walked to the mission hall soon after the fire, she discovered many of the people had found refuge on the sidewalks, around the hall she was renting—under cardboard, tin, or whatever could be found to make a roof over their heads. The opportunity to share the Gospel with these people was literally "at our doorstep."

Missionary colleagues called her Auntie Mun, and our Chinese co-workers called her Mrs. Mun. This name was derived from her Chinese name. From Auntie Mun's apartment window she could look out on all the activity as the Hong Kong government cleared the burned-out areas and built many two-story temporary housing structures. God burdened her heart for all those people who had lost everything. She remembered the 100 pounds of gospel tracts in Chinese the Pilgrim Tract Society had sent. With the workers who had come, they began systematically to pass out the gospel tracts to everyone in that area. Auntie Mun said, "For the first time in three months my heart is at ease regarding the Christmas fire victims. No longer do the ashes of a burnt village or the rude huts off the streets haunt me. They are behind, and out there before me lies the new with tremendous possibilities. This is our contribution to the fire victims. Peter said to the lame man, 'Silver and gold have I none; but such as I have give I thee.' What a privilege is ours of reaching 10,000 homes with the glorious Gospel of Jesus Christ!"[5]

Highlights of the first years from November 1953-1958 were like building blocks for the future. Under Rev. Woods, who was also the field director for Taiwan, and Mrs. Munroe, the OMS Hong Kong work was established. Several former seminary students from Canton, South China, who had fled to Hong Kong and Macau, were contacted and they joined the team. Rooms were rented on the 12th floor of a high-rise building on Taipo Road for our offices. The first two churches were opened and under a new government plan, OMS registered three rooftop schools.

Rev. Ho and family.

Rev. Ho baptizing a believer in the new church baptistry.

Mrs. Florence Munroe and Rev. Robert Erny, with some of the first Chinese Co-workers.

CHAPTER 3

EARLY CO-WORKERS
REV. HO YUI CHI – GOD'S MAN
1953-1976

Some of the first Chinese staff were former students from the OMS Bible Seminary in Canton who had escaped to Hong Kong. Ho Yui Chi was the only one of his family to escape from China. He had gone to Macau, the tiny Portuguese colony, about 40 miles from Hong Kong. Mr. Siu, translator of the Oriental Missionary Society's *Revival Magazine*, had invited him to come and be the editor of the magazine. The English material came from OMS in India written by Dr. Eugene Erny, Dr. Wesley Duewel, and others. Work on the *Revival Magazine* continued from Hong Kong, and Rev. So Tin Wong did the translation. Many of about 8,000 copies of each monthly edition were mailed to Mainland China addresses as well as foreign countries. This was a wonderful magazine addressing spiritual issues. A young believer who was willing to persevere to understand the articles could find much help. Tang Sun Chuen, one of the early co-workers still active in the Hong Kong Evangelical Church, recalled these thoughts.

Four years later in late 1953, Mr. Ho received a telegram from Mrs. Monroe, his former teacher in the Canton Bible Seminary, asking him to come to Hong Kong and help her. Mr. Ho lacked one semester of graduating from the

OMS Seminary in Canton, when it closed because of World War II.

A shy man, Mr. Ho was smaller than most Chinese with nothing particular to set him apart. In an interview Mr. Tang said of him: "Mr. Ho made an indelible impression on my life. He was a thin little man, but he was very faithful and a powerful preacher. His countenance was that of a serious man. Like his Master, there was nothing about his appearance to attract you to him."

However, when Mr. Ho shared his testimony of God's power and guidance, he radiated God's love. This is from his testimony:

I had the great fortune of being born into a Christian home. From my earliest years, I heard the Word of God read and took part in family devotions. But it was not until high school that I truly accepted Christ as my Savior. When war broke out with Japan and the enemy moved threateningly near our home, I fled to Hong Kong, thinking to find protection under the British flag. But then that dreadful day came when in December 1941, Hong Kong was attacked. During the long, terrible night which followed, I was more frightened than I had ever been in my life. I cried out, "Oh God, I belong to you. If you take my life, it is all right; but if you spare me, I will offer myself for your service." That night God kept me safe.

God was preparing his heart for pastoral ministry and future leadership of the Hong Kong Evangelical Church.

Rev. Ho went to Tokyo, Japan, in 1967 as the delegate from the Hong Kong Evangelical Church for the

Conference of the Asian-OMS related churches. When he returned, he showed us something that meant so much to him. One of the Japanese brothers had given Rev. Ho his old Bible and a picture of his family and promised to pray for Rev. Ho. This small man who struggled with feelings of inferiority because of a poor voice and a weak body was becoming a giant for the Lord. More of his testimony will show how he thought:

God spoke to me through His Word. The verse was 1 Thessalonians 2:4, "But just as we have been approved by God to be entrusted with the gospel, so we speak, not to please men, but to please God who tests our hearts." This strengthened my faith; and I decided to enter seminary. Since then this passage has been the cornerstone of my ministry.

Rev. Ho was the first pastor of the First Church, later Grace Light Church. When he preached, he could make the Scriptures relevant to our needs. In a letter Mrs. Munroe wrote:

One Sunday evening in December 1957, Mr. Ho preached. For one illustration he used the visit of Jesus to the home of Mary, Martha, and Lazarus in Bethany. He pointed out that Martha showed unusually good sense in frankly airing her complaint to the Master, rather than waiting until He had gone and then giving vent to her injured feelings by giving Mary a good scolding. The point? Family quarrels could be averted by first spreading the whole affair before the Lord in prayer.

13

Another interesting happening in Mr. Ho's life was his courtship with Lin Pui Ying. Mr. Tang, who later became the best man at their wedding, remembers those days:

At that time, there were many street meetings and some seminary students were invited to help. Miss Lin Pui Ying was one of them. She had just graduated from the Hong Kong Bible School and was interning in the church for about three months. After the internship she continued to work in the church. Because Mr. Ho and Miss Lin had many chances to work together, they later fell in love. Miss Lin had a great struggle in her heart because Mr. Ho was ten years older. He was serious and quiet and she was active and sociable. Her family and some friends were not happy about this relationship and had other ideas for her. She had a difficult decision to make.

The church prayed for them while Rev. McClain and Mrs. Munroe encouraged them and helped them. Because of their differences many thought they wouldn't get married. However, they had a common goal in their lives. They wanted to serve God, work for the church, and preach the Gospel. They were finally married in 1961.

Mrs. Ho Lin Pui Ying became the Bible woman for the church and worked alongside her husband for many years until his death from cancer in August 1976. They had two children, a boy and girl, and God has taken care of them through the years. Their son, Mr. Ho Chung Kwong (Praise Light), married one of the young ladies from Grace Rock Church, and their daughter married also.

After Rev. Ho was gone, Mrs. Ho told the Hong Kong Evangelical Church Conference that her husband wanted her to carry on the work of the church just as they had planned together. This she did very capably and received her ordination in April 1979. As is the custom of the Chinese women, they use their maiden name even after they are married. So Mrs. Ho, known to everyone as Rev. Lin Pui Ying, ministered in Grace Rock Church until she emigrated to the United States to pastor a Chinese church in the Midwest.

STEPHEN YIK KAI NIN

Rev. Ho had met a young man in Macau while he was working on the *Revival Magazine*. Mr.Yik Kai Nin, or Stephen, lived in Macau and attended the South China Holiness Church where he had been baptized. Rev. E. R. Munroe had gone to China under this church and eventually asked OMS to take over the China work. Rev. Ho knew this church and had a connection. Stephen Yik had graduated from high school and, because he didn't have a job, volunteered to help on the magazine. When Mrs. Munroe asked Rev. Ho to come to Hong Kong, he persuaded Stephen to come too. Mrs. Munroe urged Stephen to attend the Bethel Seminary in Kowloon City, which he did from 1955 to 1958. Stephen did a variety of things within OMS and the church. He taught at OMS Bible Seminary when it began and interpreted for missionaries and visiting preachers. He loved music and helped with music in some of the rooftop schools and chapel services. In 1964 Stephen went to Azusa Pacific College in California, returning to Hong Kong in early 1966. He continued helping in the church and with OMS until he went back to Azusa for further studies.

15

Stephen married Pauline Lei, daughter of Rev. Lei Hang On, who was captain of the ECC team and one of our faithful pastors. They went to Taiwan where Stephen and Pauline were much involved at our OMS Chung Tai Theological Seminary in Tai Chung. They moved to Los Angeles and it was later found that their son, Leo, a young man, had a brain tumor. The surgery to remove the tumor left Leo disabled, making it necessary for Pauline and their daughter to continue to live in L.A. to care for him. After Leo's condition stabilized somewhat, Stephen went back to Taiwan to teach in the seminary. Later Stephen assisted in Hong Kong with the opening of the Wesleyan United Graduate Institute in the fall of 2000. This couple has been through much suffering, but they let God continue to use them.

REV. WONG YUK NAN
CHAUFFEUR FOR THE LORD

"Brother, you are trying to talk price with God and that will never do." The pastor's voice was gentle but stern as he talked with Mr. Wong Yuk Nan. Mr. Wong had lots of problems in his life and some evil habits. He didn't really want to yield to the Lord. He tried to compromise with God. If God would heal his son, then . . . The pastor explained that God does not come at our beck and call but wants us to come to Him in humility, repentance, and trust. Mr. Wong finally surrendered to Jesus. He closed his unscrupulous business and went to work digging ditches and hard manual labor. He was surprised to find that his bad habits, which he thought would be so hard to break, just slipped from him and were gone. He was indeed a new man.[6]

A year after his conversion, Mr. Wong became the official driver of OMS' first Volkswagen Micro-Bus, helping Mrs. Munroe and other staff members get around more quickly. He had done this work in the army and enjoyed nothing better, always wearing a big smile as he drove. The Wongs were also in the first group to be baptized in October 1954.

Mr. and Mrs. Wong had four children when she was diagnosed as being in the first stages of tuberculosis. The doctor advised complete rest with medical treatments. A month or so later, Mrs. Wong was improving, but they learned that their eight-month-old baby girl also had the disease. Many prayed for this dear family, and God healed both Mrs. Wong and the baby.

Chinese Christians celebrate every anniversary of the beginning of our OMS church in Hong Kong, often very creatively. At the third anniversary in February 1957, six ladies competed for prizes in a contest in which they recited scripture verses. The first lady was one of the rooftop teachers with a good memory. She began in Genesis taking verses here and there through the Bible until she reached Revelation. She gave 105 verses with their correct locations. When the second contestant was called, who should come to the platform but the chauffeur's wife, Mrs. Wong. Where did she find the time to memorize Scripture? She had four growing children and only a fifth grade education. Before she finished, she had recited 85 verses. Another older lady came who had taught herself to read the Bible. She had memorized 57 verses. Amazingly, she could only read the Bible and not other literature. What glory to God!

Mr. Wong began to sense the Lord calling him to the ministry of winning souls for Jesus Christ. He gave up being chauffeur and spent one year with the Every Creature Crusade before going to seminary and pastoring one of the rooftop congregations. Later, Rev. Wong helped begin the chapel at Tai Po Market.

HOLLY WONG LEUNG

Holly was a high schooler and in my very first English Bible class held in the first Yan Kwong Chapel on Apliu Street. As the Wongs' daughter, she has the distinction that many of the rest of us have—being a preacher's kid! She grew up knowing some of the hardships of the early years in Hong Kong as well as sensing the heartache and pain of her parents when her little brother, their precious and only son, became very ill. Holly struggled with the issue of giving her heart wholly to Jesus until she was 17 years old, when she made that commitment to the Lord.

Wanting to help people, Holly took nurses training. Upon her graduation she worked in a hospital, but she was increasingly aware that God wanted her to do more in full time evangelism and discipling. She resigned from her job and went to the Evangelical Free Church Seminary in Hong Kong.

While working as a nurse, she met Derek Leung at their church. Derek asked her to marry him, but Holly wasn't ready for marriage. She knew that she had more Bible training than Derek did, and she wanted him to be the spiritual leader in their home. What Holly didn't know was that Derek was taking night Bible classes. After three years of study, he again asked Holly to marry him and she did in 1976, around the time she began working with Marilyn Snider in children's work.

Holly has worked with the Hong Kong Evangelical Church and with OMS. For many years now she has been teaching Bible at United Christian College and filling in when needed as school nurse. When asked whether she and Derek were planning to emigrate to another country, Holly said she plans to continue as Bible teacher and counselor at UCC for as long as she can.

"Since what happens to the Christians in the future is completely out of our hands," she said, "why waste time worrying about it? My priority is to train young people to be strong in their faith so that whatever comes they'll stand firm and true to God."

Holly and Derek have one daughter, Karen, who at this writing is almost finished with her studies at Hong Kong University. She also wants to use her life to help people.

These dear co-workers are preparing to suffer for their faith and to that end are reading many books written by Chinese Christians who have already suffered for Jesus Christ. Holly said that she tries to stay close to the Lord through praying, reading the Bible, and asking God to give her scriptures that will help her be strong. [7]

Dorothy and Holly Wong Leung. Holly is now the school nurse at United Christian College and teaches Bible classes.

A special program for the children on one of the OMS rooftop schools.

A Bible class for the children in a rooftop school.

CHAPTER 4

THE FLEDGLING CHURCH

The first church began in the mission hall in Sham Shui Po where Auntie Mun had found a space for the people to worship. She recalls after some months the numbers grew so much that three people had to sit on two chairs and others had to sit or stand outside on the sidewalk. The church was located on Apliu Street, which means "duck coop." Before the city limits had taken in this section, it was a large duck farm, giving the street its name. Walking up and down the street and seeing plenty of what looks like coops, one might think that ducks still lived there. In the early days people, not ducks, lived in them—people who had met with disasters and lost everything. What looks like rows of coops are now places for small entrepreneurs to store their goods.

One would also see row after row of empty steel drums, stacks of old metal pieces, old tires, greasy shops with young men working on cars, and men and women sewing up the famous red, white and blue heavy plastic China bags—a must for missionaries to store stuff in! The bags got their name from thousands of people who fill them full of goods for their families and carry them into China.

In this area of the city the ministry of preaching the Gospel to the multitude of refugee Chinese was born. Friends at home read the following article about the opening of the

OMS work in Hong Kong in the mission magazine, *Missionary Standard* (now named the *OMS Outreach*):

ANNOUNCING THE ARRIVAL OF THE LATEST MEMBER OF THE ORIENTAL MISSIONARY SOCIETY FAMILY

Date: 2 P.M., February 27, 1954
Name: Hong Kong
Size: Larger than its cradle

Although healthy and perfectly normal, it will be sometime before this child will be able to stand on its own feet or help itself. We are giving it plenty of the "sincere milk of the Word," and have no doubt but what the time will soon come when it will be able to take meat and grow tall, like Samuel who had a new coat every year. In the meantime it will need all the help and support we are able to give it. We can say, with Hannah, "For this child I prayed; and the Lord hath given me my petition which I asked of him."

--F. Munroe

On October 31, 1954, the first baptismal service took place at First Church, when Rev. Uri Chandler, an OMS missionary from Taiwan, baptized 48 believers. They ranged in age from a little 10-year-old girl to a 75-year-old brother and ranked in social standing from a street sweeper to a college professor. Mutual sufferings and the grace of God, however, wiped out all class distinction. In Calvary love and victory, they found one common ground of fellowship and their hearts were knit together as brothers and sisters in the Lord. They are a precious group—these first fruits of the work in Hong Kong.

February 27, 1955, marked the first anniversary of opening the Oriental Missionary Society work in Hong Kong. What a thrill for OMS Director Harry Woods to baptize 22 more believers.

SECOND CHURCH OPENED – REV. & MRS. PETER LAW

1954-65

In July 1955, the second mission hall opened in Sham Shui Po on Poplar Street with the help of Peter Law. Peter had studied in the OMS Seminary in Shanghai, and his wife was one of Auntie Mun's adopted Chinese daughters. Mrs. Law came to help first and talked Auntie Mun into asking her husband to help open the second mission hall. Peter was working in another place at the time. Their children were grown allowing them to give full-time work to this new ministry. They started with 55 charter members. The Laws visited some of the refugees living in a nearby squatters' village and prayed that the Lord would help them reach those people. Then another awful fire swept through that village taking its toll. When Mrs. Munroe went to the new mission hall the next night, she saw people all around the hall living on the sidewalk. The people were from the village they had prayed for, and now here they were by the doorstep of the mission. After just three months they had 60 people in a class preparing for baptism.[8]

REV. NG YUE TONG

1956-1980

Ng Yue Tong was a soldier far from home when the Communist army swept down from the north. His only alternative was to flee to Hong Kong. He dared not go back, and his young wife could not get a permit to come to Hong Kong. That was in 1949. This story was repeated over and over as different ones came to know the Lord Jesus in our chapels. As we became acquainted with them and learned about their families, we were able to help and encourage them. So many lost everything as they fled to freedom.

We met Mr. Ng shortly after our second mission hall was opened. He accepted the Lord, which radically changed his life. In the fall of 1956, he joined the teaching staff of the second rooftop school. Then responding to God's call, he entered the seminary when it began in early 1958. Mr. Ng began to pray for the release of his wife from behind the Bamboo Curtain, and after three years she was able to join him in Hong Kong. Some time later, after an acute attack of tuberculosis, Mrs. Ng was willing to give her heart to the Lord. We were thankful that this little family, which now included a daughter, was together and following the Lord Jesus Christ.

Rev. Ng was eventually assigned to pastor the second church, Grace Showers or Yan Yue Church. This was the church where he found the Lord years before and where the Laws had ministered. By that time the Laws had emigrated to the United States to be with their daughter, Helen Law.[9]

CHAPTER 5

H-BLOCK BUILDINGS AND
OUR FIRST SCHOOLS

In late 1954 the government had begun construction of H-block resettlement buildings. These seven-story structures were built to house the hundreds of thousands of refugee squatters whose huts covered the hillsides and clogged the sidewalks. Each building housed about 2,500 persons in tiny rooms ten by 12 feet, a minimum of five adults in one cubicle. Children under ten years of age counted as one half of an adult. We had a woman who came to the clinic with high blood pressure and lots of headaches. She had nine children in that little cubicle with her. Auntie Mun often said, "Pause and think of that!" The part that made the huge "H" crossbar was the water and toilet facilities for all the people of each floor. Many built locked boxes for their cooking utensils in the narrow corridor that circled the entire floor. The flat tops of these seven-story structures were enclosed with heavy wire fencing and had some covering on each end.

From the very beginning the children held a special place in Mrs. Munroe's heart. These little ones, who lived with their parents on the sidewalks and wherever they could find a space, had no place to play or to go to school. In the first chapel on Apliu Street, Auntie Mun decided to have a Sunday school. More than 200 children, eager to learn, came the first Sunday. The next morning the whole crowd was there again gathered about the door of the mission hall, ready for another Sunday school. Thus began the daily Bible classes for the children.

Mrs. Munroe approached the government with the idea that the flat tops of the H-block buildings could be used as a place for the children to play, and the covered rooms at each end could be for classes. With the help of her housekeeper, Auntie Mun accomplished the first major step in securing permission for the schools. A relative of the housekeeper was a Christian and an official in the new housing area at Tai Hang Tung, where the fires had destroyed so much. His instructions soon placed her formal application in the hands of the right department to grant the request. In less than a month, the government granted permission for the large rooftop with 7,500 square feet (1,400 square feet of that under shelter) to be used as a school. In July 1955 the school began with over 300 students, morning and afternoons, with additional classes in the evening for adults. All the teachers for this school had accepted Jesus as their Savior through the ministry of the First Church. Previously they had been teachers in China or had held other responsible positions.[10]

Our first rooftop school was so successful that in May 1956 we were granted another rooftop in the Lei Cheng Uk Resettlement Village. By the fall this rooftop school was in operation with 300 children enrolled for religious instruction every day. An estimated 30,000 to 40,000 people lived in this area. What a wonderful privilege!

In the early days most of the rooftop was open. More space needed to be enclosed so that all the children would have a covered place to sit for their lessons. In one of Auntie Mun's letters, I found this wonderful picture of the need for more cover. Hong Kong had been suffering drought for many months and water had been rationed. Here is her report:

Friday morning, 150 boys and girls were gathered under a shelter at one end of the long rooftop to listen and to watch a flannelgraph Bible story. A black cloud was hovering low, but we were entirely unprepared for the terrific storm that suddenly broke upon us—a wild deluge of rain driven by semi-hurricane winds. The canvas around the enclosure was blown hither and thither. The rain beat in upon us with terrible violence, while the lightening flashed and thunders rolled. For the next few minutes pandemonium reigned! There was a wild skirmish as 150 children vied with one another for standing room on a spot in the center that alone bore the semblance of what one would call dry.

"We're all wet! Our books are soaked!" came the piteous wail of childish voices. I must confess that, for the moment, I lost my poise completely. Then above the roar of the storm and the din of childish voices, a sharp whistle sounded, and Mr. Yip, our principal, was suddenly beside me. Almost instantly the sound of voices ceased while 150 pairs of terrified eyes were fixed upon him. "Who is causing it to rain?" shouted Mr. Yip, making a trumpet of his

27

hands. There was a slight pause and then the answer came back clear and strong, "The Heavenly Father."

"Have you not been asking Him for rain?" And as the answer came back in the affirmative, frightened looks gave way to sheepish grins. "I know your backs are wet and your books are soaked, but if this is the Heavenly Father's will for us, should we be displeased about it?" Then while the storm raged on for an hour or more, Mr. Yip kept those boys and girls with their attention riveted upon him as he told them of the Father's love and care for us and how the big reservoirs were filling up, inch by inch. "Why, maybe we can have water twice a day now. Won't that be wonderful!"

Then, cleverly using the storm for a setting for the story of Jonah at sea, he continued to keep the children so interested that they seemed to forget their present situation—wet backs and all—until the storm had abated enough for them to get home safely and into dry clothing. I came away thanking the Lord for Mr. Yip, but wondering if wet backs and soaked books were indeed the Father's will for those children. Maybe the Lord let the tempest strike to show us how badly we do need the enclosures and to prod us on to more faith to believe Him for our needs. "Lord, I believe, help thou my unbelief."[11]

CHAPTER 6

THE TEACHERS

REV. & MRS. YIP CHIU MING

Mr. & Mrs. Yip Chiu Ming were among some of the first to come to Jesus in our mission hall and were in the first group to be baptized. Mr. Yip had held a good position in China before 1949 and was a university graduate. Due to the political change in China, they were compelled to leave everything and seek refuge in Hong Kong. With what money they had, they began a small business. They were doing fairly well until they, too, were caught in a fire that left the family destitute. They were assigned to a small place on the sidewalk, which became their home.

Just around the corner from their home was the OMS mission hall. Mrs. Yip and the children came first, and Mrs. Yip sought and found the Lord. Mr. Yip saw the change in her and his oldest daughter, and the peace and joy that they had found. Soon his daughter showed him the way to Jesus and he, too, became a believer. Later on Mrs. Munroe invited Mr. Yip to be in charge of the educational ministry, as he had been in that work before they left China. He also had a burden for the children.

They soon became active in the work of the church. Mr. and Mrs. Yip said they found so much joy in serving the Lord that they did not regret the loss of all their worldly possessions. They felt that if these reverses had never come to them, they might not have found the Savior. Verses 71 and 75 of Psalm 119 say, *It was good for me to be afflicted so that I might learn your decrees; I know, O Lord, that your laws are righteous, and in faithfulness you have afflicted me.*

The rooftop school was the avenue the Lord gave to reach the children, both with knowledge of the Lord Jesus and with practical education. We were ready to open our second rooftop and we needed a capable man in charge. A year earlier a man had come to know Jesus as Savior in one of the summer services, but we hadn't seen him for some time. He might be the man. The Lord directed Pastor Ho in writing a letter to Mr. Hui. If he was the Lord's man, then we would hear from him.

REV. HUI MAK LAM

Yes, the Lord brought Hui Mak Lam to us, and what a wonderful addition! His story is like so many others who had to run for their lives and leave everything, including family, six years earlier. Mr. Hui, fleeing for his life, knew the only way to be safe was to reach the British colony of Hong Kong. With the Communists closing in, he did not even have time to notify his wife and children. The provincial Senate, of which he was secretary, suddenly dissolved in confusion. His home and family were miles away in the opposite direction from Hong Kong. It would be suicide to try to reach them.

In Hong Kong, Mr. Hui eked out an existence—sometimes doing manual labor, sometimes working at a desk. The smelly fish market supplied him with a menial job for a while, but he hated it. He had heard during that hot summer in 1955 about Jesus forgiving His tormentors. With too much bitterness eating in his heart, how could he forgive? But sitting in the chapel that day, before the service was finished, Mr. Hui opened his heart to Jesus. He experienced a peace and rest in his heart he never dreamed one could have.

Later Mr. Hui asked for a private interview with Mrs. Munroe. When he came in, he seemed serious and nervous. Quickly getting to the point, he said, "Mrs. Mun, do you know there is a woman who wants to come and live with me?" She gasped and thought, what scandal this is! But his next words cleared the situation. "I told her she must become a Christian before I could marry her. She was baptized last Sunday. With your consent we would like to arrange for the wedding before school begins."

For more than a year Mr. Hui had been ably directing the work on our second rooftop at Lei Cheng Uk Estate. As we talked of plans for his wedding, Mr. Hui told me how his wife's younger sister had escaped from Communist China some months before. She brought the first news of his family he had had in seven years. His wife had long since been dead. Relatives were caring for his children, but because of the scarcity of food, it was unlikely they would survive long. His sister-in-law had readily accepted the Lord as her Savior, and she was the one he planned to marry.

After his marriage Mr. Hui responded to the call of God to prepare for the ministry. Already a university graduate, he took his place among high school graduates in the OMS Bible Seminary and received his diploma in 1961.[12]

The year before, we had opened our fourth and largest rooftop school in the Wong Tai Sin Resettlement Estates. Rev. Hui was appointed to organize and take charge, not only of the school, which was called Bamboo Gardens, but also of the evangelistic work. How we praised God when Zion Church (Yan Shek) became the first organized church on the rooftop.

Rev. Robert Erny, Hong Kong field director, wrote an article for the *Missionary Standard* in February 1971, where he tells of a "Miracle in Ward E-3":

Mr. Hui Mak Lam had been given the final diagnosis after trips to one specialist after another. This was shared only by Mrs. Hui and myself, that Mr. Hui had inoperable brain cancer. I had prayed with him; I had prayed for him. I had struggled to believe, to pray for the impossible—that a man with brain cancer should live. "Lord," I pleaded, "You are Almighty; You can do all things. Heal Rev. Hui." We had talked about Pastor Hui in somber tones. Who would take his place? Pastor his church? He was one of our finest men. Then this! The moment I walked through the door he was out of bed, walking slowly, carefully towards me. "Oh, Pastor Erny," his words and his face beamed a welcome. "I have been hoping you would come today." Pastor Hui began then to tell of all he had experienced. It was the first time since the onset of his illness that his speech was intelligible. Now the words came out slowly and clearly, round and deep. "God has been so good to me; I cannot thank Him enough."

I have thought a good deal," Hui continued, "wondering why God has been so good to me. Certainly it is not because of my own faith or worthiness. I am sure it can only be because of prayer. Someone prayed. I know you have prayed for me." He was looking at me now, eyes filled with gratitude, but I knew it was not due to my faith. "And our fellow workers and many believers in our churches have prayed."

The visiting hour was up. I said goodbye to Pastor Hui and walked out of the hospital. Some deep inner part of my being was shaken. The incandescent light of God's revelation to Hui had somehow erased the ordinary distinction between life and death. I recognized, perhaps more deeply than ever before, that to glorify God, either by life or by death, is all that really counts. What does it matter if Hui's physical healing is for a few months or a few years? What is life except a moment-by-moment preparing to meet God? The great miracle that had taken place was the healing of Hui's soul.

Six months have passed since Pastor Hui left the hospital. He has had many opportunities to give his testimony, and each time God has received much glory. Several days ago Pastor Hui was in to see me. I asked him about his arm. "Oh, the doctor said it was nothing to worry about," he replied. But then he added with a quiet smile, "Of course, I know it is the cancer still in my body, but I am not afraid. God has already answered my prayer. I have been able to bring glory to His name. I did not ask for more than that." Rev. Hui Mak Lam went to be with the Lord October 1, 1971. He had been plagued with the cancer since May 1970.

REV. & MRS. LEE CHI YIU

Another couple who came from China as refugees without anything, Mr. and Mrs. Lee Chi Yiu, eventually found their way into our OMS Chapel. This is a part of their testimony published in an article in the *Missionary Standard* in December 1959:

> *We fled Red China leaving three children with their grandparents. They are teenagers now. The ministry of the OMS introduced us to Jesus Christ. We are refugees who have found The Refuge! Our greatest heartbreak is that our three children, ages 18, 16, and 13 years, have never known us as Christian parents. Now that we are Christians, our minds and hearts are deeply burdened by the awful knowledge that our children's minds are being poisoned by the deadly diet of godless Communism. Won't you pray for them?*

From Mrs. Munroe's *Harbor Of Hope* there is much more to the Lees' testimony:

> *Mr. and Mrs. Lee, with a small daughter, fled their home together. Two sons and a daughter had to be left behind. I don't remember ever meeting a woman more despondent than Mrs. Lee. The shack in which they lived, together with all they possessed, was burned to ashes. They, with others, were sent to live on the sidewalk.*

34

Mr. Lee found work, but it was across the bay on the island part of the city. His long hours made it impossible for him to get home except on weekends. Mrs. Lee had nothing to do but to sit in a hovel and grieve for her children and lost relatives. Both had come from wealthy homes and knew what it was to have plenty; now they were barely existing.

It was through the witness of his sister that Mr. Lee came to the mission and gave his heart to the Lord. Mrs. Lee soon followed—and what a change! As it dawned upon her that God actually answers the prayers of His children, she began to pray and believe for an answer—and the answers came! The list runs something like this: One, they were soon moved from the sidewalk to a room in a resettlement area. Two, to their great joy, a little son was given them. Three, both Mr. and Mrs. Lee were given places on our teaching staff, and now he could live at home. Four, Mr. Lee, stricken down with tuberculosis (a result of the strenuous work in which he had formerly been engaged) was given free hospitalization and treatments for a year and was pronounced cured. Five, Mr. Lee was called of the Lord to preach and entered the seminary soon after it was opened in 1958.

By this time, Mrs. Lee was sure that "with God nothing is impossible." She began asking Him to release her three children. "I'm so busy praying for things that I don't have time to worry or to be sad any more," she would say. She was a real tonic to all of us. Did her children get out? Yes!

Mr. and Mrs. Lee both were able to join the first OMS seminary class in early 1958. It was held in the afternoons, as most of the workers who were studying were also teaching on the rooftops. They studied eight courses: The Gospels, Doctrine, Bible History, Bible Geography, Personal Work, Sunday School Methods, English, and Music. Mrs. Lee was a busy woman with two children to care for, the rooftop ministry, seminary classes, and her studies. In one of her reports she said:

Personally, I feel my dependence upon the Lord, for I do not feel adequate for my responsibilities. I feel weak spiritually and in my teaching of all those under me. However, I do trust in the Lord's power for He reminds us in the Bible, "My grace is sufficient for thee, for my strength is made perfect in weakness." This is of great comfort and encourages me.[13]

The following short testimony was taken from one of Mr. Lee's prayer letters:

When it was determined that I had TB and would have to go to the hospital for treatment, I was in great despair. I was tempted to blame God, thinking He had forsaken me and let this calamity befall me even while I was training in the Bible Seminary for His service. I did not know this was His way of correction for me. Afterward the Holy Spirit spoke to my heart and then I understood that because He loved me He had provided this time set aside to be quiet and draw

36

near to Him. When I confessed my sin, my heart was filled with comfort.

I was worrying about my sickness for I feared I might have to be operated upon. At that time God spoke to me through Psalm 27:1—"The Lord is my light and my salvation; whom shall I fear? The Lord is the stronghold of my life, of whom shall I be afraid?" When He gave me this precious Word, my heart was filled with peace and joy. I took myself to Him and He has strengthened me.

In the late '70s we closed down the rooftop school at Lei Ching Uk and after that the Lees emigrated to Canada to be near their children. In a Christmas card in 1998, came the word from Mr. Lee that Mrs. Lee went to be with the Lord March 17, 1998. She was 83 years old.

REV. SO TIN WONG

During 1956, Rev. So Tin Wong joined the staff. He came well equipped for a seminary ministry as teacher, interpreter, and translator. With Rev. So's help we began some evening classes on a seminary level. He came to the OMS with a wealth of experience and having known the Lord for many years. He studied in a seminary in Canton and then later was invited to go to New Zealand to preach to the Chinese there. He went back to Canton, China, where he worked for a large church denomination as a book translator and a Bible teacher until the Sino-Japanese war broke out. During the war he taught in a senior high school to earn money in order to preach. When the Communists took over Canton in 1949, Rev. So came to Hong Kong where he found OMS and worked with us for many years. His wife and one daughter were in Hong Kong, but his two sons and two daughters-in-law and seven grandchildren could not get out of China. When the Communists persecuted several of his family to death, Rev. So had much deep sorrow, which deepened when his mother was persecuted and died at the age of 86.

In 1963, my first year in Hong Kong, Rev. So, the oldest of our pastors, bestowed on me a beautiful Chinese name—beautiful and a challenge to live up to. My name, Baak Louh Geet, means *white and pure as the dew*. He thought that the sounds were close to my name, Dorothy Backer. I will always remember a very kind, soft-spoken, white-haired Chinese gentleman. The Chinese love to have a good meaning in a name, and I am grateful for the name and the man who gave it to me.

Rev. Yip Chiu Ming on left with his wife, Mrs. Yip and Mr. Tang Sun Chuen.

38

Rev. Hui Mak Lam, his wife and little girl. He married the sister of his first wife who died in China.

Rev. Lei Chi Yu and Mrs. Lei.
(All these knew suffering, yet rejoiced in Christ, their Savior.)

Rev. Lee Hobel and family were some of the first missionaries who came to help Mrs. Munroe. They taught on the rooftops and were involved in evangelism.

Rev. Dale and Polly McClain with children, Carol, Richard, and Doug when they arrived in Hong Kong in 1957.

CHAPTER 7

ARRIVAL OF NEW MISSIONARIES

In September 1955 missionaries Lee and Helen Hobel and their two little boys, David and Stephen, arrived in Hong Kong aboard the S.S. Anna Bakke. Settling in was difficult because of the heat and there had been little rain for several months. Besides working on learning Cantonese, they were involved in evangelism and teaching on the rooftops. They celebrated David's fourth birthday on March 15, 1956, Stephen's second birthday on March 16, and on March 19 everyone welcomed little Mark Allen Hobel into the missionary family, the newest one. Mrs. Munroe was very glad to have some helpers in the great task of sharing Jesus Christ with the Chinese people.

In a prayer letter from Auntie Mun written in March 1956, she tells of Easter Sunday:

During the month of March we examined, one by one, 82 candidates for baptism. The testimonies and experiences of these new Christians would make an interesting book of no little size. The majority of them are refugees from inside China and know what it is to endure hard things.

Our director, Rev. Harry F. Woods, was with us. On the last Sunday of March and the first Sunday of April, he baptized the group of new converts mentioned above. He preached almost every night during the week and sometimes twice a day. Easter Sunday was our Red Letter day. It began with an early morning service for all the Christians and was held on the rooftop of the seven-story building in Tai Hang Tung (the first rooftop school). At 11 a.m., Communion was served to a large group in the first church. At two o'clock, 55 believers, the fruits of nine months' labor in the new mission, were baptized, and the second OMS church in Hong Kong was organized with 60 charter members. Later, Communion was also served to this group. The service continued through till 5:30; then all these new members ate rice together. By 8:30, the evening service was in progress, and thus closed a very eventful day for many.

REV. DALE MCCLAIN –
FIRST FIELD DIRECTOR
1957-1965 & 1984-87

In August 1957, Rev. Dale and Pauline McClain with their three children—Carol, Richard, and Douglas—arrived to join Mrs. Munroe and the Hobels. The McClains had previously served in Canton, China. Polly's parents, Orville and Aileen French, were OMS missionaries in Korea and China in the late '20s and '30s. When China's doors closed, Dale and Polly went to India. Polly had been very ill in India, and their missionary career on foreign soil seemed to be ended. But God worked a miracle in their lives and after five years was moving them to Hong Kong for ministry. Already having some knowledge of the Cantonese language, they were quickly busy in ministry. Preaching, teaching, and Bible studies took much of their time. The children attended a British Primary School in Kowloon. Eventually Carol went to Taichung, Taiwan, to attend Morrison Academy, a high school for missionary kids using the American system.

Under Dale's leadership, from 1958-1965, the seminary began, as many of the early workers wanted to know more about the Bible. They were the first students. The Every Creature Crusade began in Hong Kong, and two churches were formed with these teams. The vision to have our own center in Kowloon was born, and Dale saw the construction and opening of Chung Yan Primary School. Dale also saw the Kau Yan Medical Center built and opened, and work on the church had begun before Dale and Polly left for the USA in 1965.

MARY ELLEN BEETLEY,
FIRST FULL-TIME SECRETARY
1958-1987

With the increased responsibilities of the seminary, more help was needed. Mary Ellen Beetley arrived December 23, 1958, to be Dale's secretary. By this time Dale was also the field director. Mary Ellen had worked with Dale in the homeland in the Men For Missions office, then at Winona Lake, Indiana. Her skills in the office were a real help. Besides her secretarial abilities, she was the bookkeeper for many years. She also had musical talent and through the years played the piano in several of the churches, taught piano to the young people so they could help their own church music ministry, taught English classes, and shared Christ with the people. The young people really loved her. She had a tremendous ministry of listening and praying for and with her piano students. Only Heaven will tell the fruit of those times.

Mary Ellen used to tell about the rickety elevator they had to take up to the OMS office on the 11th floor of Wah Kiu Mansion on Tai Po Road. Sometimes it would be overloaded and get stuck between floors. She hated that, but patience won out and eventually the elevator would slowly creep to the right floor. The OMS Seminary was on the floor above the office, and a church pastored by Rev. Lei Hang On met there on Sundays for a while. The church was later merged with Yan Kwong Church.

Another memory of Mary Ellen's was that Auntie Mun lived in part of the office apartment and sometimes would make snacks for them. She recalled the broiled squid that tasted pretty good—then!

Mary Ellen suddenly entered heaven's gates May 6, 1997, at the age of 71. She was such a great source of remembering things about the early days in Hong Kong, and so many times I have wanted to call her and ask if she remembered someone's name or a particular event. How glorious that she is now sharing with many of the co-workers who have gone on before.

The OMS office was still on Tai Po Road when I arrived in September 1963. I recall taking that rickety elevator and also recall lots of laughter while squeezed together in the tiny space. I also remember that was the place of the Saturday prayer meetings for all the workers. Kneeling in prayer for more than an hour on thin little pads, listening to loud buzzing—at least that is what Cantonese sounded like to me at that time—was an endurance test for some of us "greenies." But I haven't forgotten the sounds, or the tears, or the songs of praise that came from the lips of the redeemed ones: *Jaan Mei Jyu! Jaan Mei Jyu!* Praise the Lord! Praise the Lord!

REV. ROBERT ERNY AND FAMILY
1959-1971

In October 1959 Rev. Robert and Phyllis Erny arrived, with nine-month-old Paul, to add their strengths and skills to the small missionary team. However, language study was their first assignment. Bob remembers that soon after they arrived in Hong Kong, they had to leave their little son with a Chinese helper, their new *amah* who spoke no English, and begin their first trip to language school. Learning to speak Cantonese, one of the more than 50 dialects of southern China, is very difficult. The dialect is not a written language. To learn to read, one must learn the sentence structure of Mandarin, which is the written Chinese language. It took them about an hour and a half on two buses and a ferry to get to Hong Kong University. Unfortunately, it takes about one and a half years to be able to function in the language.

Bob began to teach and help in the seminary as more students came to study. He also had to prepare a sermon with his language teacher's help, so he could use his language preaching in the chapels. Oh, the joys of learning the Chinese language!

Joy, Dan, and Ken were added to the Erny family in the years following their arrival in Hong Kong. They added much to the missionary team, and in the early years their playmates were children of some of our Chinese co-workers.

Bob directed the Hong Kong work from 1965-1971. Several things happened during those days that were somewhat discouraging, but we all knew that our God was in charge and understood why. The seminary closed because there were no students applying. Non-Christian parents did not want their sons and daughters studying there, and the family pressure was great. Much rejoicing was called for when Grace Rock Church was built. The old Yan Kwong and the small Tai Po Street Church joined and moved into the new church structure. The clinic closed in 1970 because of no doctor and spiraling medical costs. That caused some confusion in our minds because of the vision that brought it to fruition. We could not see God's greater plan—the forming of the high school for 1,200 students with the freedom to preach and teach God's Word.

Another plus was the establishment of the church, which would later be called Zion Church, on the Wong Tai Sin rooftop where we had a school. Then the Every Creature Crusade Team moved to Chuen Wan and began a chapel in that industrial section of Hong Kong.

Rev. Robert Erny came to Hong Kong in 1959. He is translating into English for Rev. Yip Chiu Ming.

CHAPTER 8

OMS OPENS A SEMINARY

God added more national workers to our team plus teachers for the children on the rooftops, but now the workers needed more training in the Bible. In 1958 Dale McClain took leadership of the newly opened Bible seminary. Our seminary was small and geared to meet the special needs of our workers. Some of the workers on the rooftop schools taught in the mornings and came to study in the seminary in the afternoon. Those who taught in the afternoon sessions took seminary classes in the mornings. In this way our early workers gained a greater knowledge of the Bible and other subjects. They studied eight courses: The Gospels, Doctrine, Bible History, Bible Geography, Personal Work, Sunday School Methods, English, and Music. The OMS Seminary in Hong Kong had been developed in conjunction with the OMS Bible Seminary in Taiwan. Almost all of our early pastors, who were so faithful and loyal through the years, came through this Bible training.

NEW SEMINARY STUDENTS/

MR. TANG SUN CHUEN

1959-1999

One of the new students who came into the seminary about the time the Ernys came was Tang Sun Chuen. Rev. Ho led him to the Lord after he had been attending the First Church for a while. He is the longest serving worker in the Hong Kong Evangelical Church, continuing to this day. He served in many capacities in the conference, from secretary and treasurer to interim pastor when needed.

Mr. Tang's story is a testimony to God's marvelous grace in his life. In 1995, I interviewed Mr. Tang and Rev. Grant Nealis translated it. This is what he said:

I want to praise the Lord. Before I believed in the Lord, I had pulmonary tuberculosis. It was quite serious. I lost weight, down to 80 pounds, and was spitting blood. I was very discouraged. Furthermore, I had lost my job and entertained thoughts of suicide.

I went to a hospital in Wanchai (Ruttonjee Sanatorium, Hong Kong Island) where the Catholic sisters examined me. As a result, I entered the sanatorium. All the patients had to help with the work. For example, some had to wash the toilets and do other odd jobs. It was so difficult for me to breathe, so most of the 100 patients in the dining room finished eating before me. After another x-ray I was told that the disease had eaten large holes in both of my lungs. I had heard that some people had surgery on their lungs and had been helped. However, due to the seriousness of my condition, I didn't want to risk surgery. This was all previous to my conversion.

I began to think about my condition. My only hope was to believe in Jesus. (At that time OMS had opened their first gospel hall—102 Apliu Street.) I began visiting various churches to hear what they had to say. When I went to the OMS church, the place where they met had nothing to commend it. The equipment was plain and simple. They didn't even have electric fans in the hot weather. But I felt the atmosphere was cordial and the people were so friendly. The pastor was Rev. Ho Yui Chi. He was a small slender man but a powerful preacher. I began to think about my spiritual condition and started giving serious consideration to believing in Jesus even though I wasn't clear as to what was involved. After reading a book from Rev. Ho, I understood that Almighty God has created the heaven and earth. He was the true God and Jesus Christ was His Son. Then I accepted Him as my Savior.

As I thought about what had happened to me, I began to realize that if my Savior could forgive my sin, He could also heal me. My faith began to grow. Tuberculosis was a very common contagious disease in Hong Kong at that time. But I started thinking that I didn't catch this disease from someone else. My illness was due to my sin. I acknowledged my sin and believed. God moved Mrs. Florence Munroe, founder of OMS-Hong Kong, to give me a menial job which paid HK$80 (US$14) per month. After two months I received HK$120 a month. This experience increased my faith to believe that God could certainly heal me. I *began to get better and my trust in God grew. God was very gracious to me. After several years, I went to see a German doctor. He told me that he feared I had tuberculosis of the bone. That made me very anxious. My heart told me, "Don't be afraid, pray." The doctor wanted me to have a special kind of x-ray, but I was determined to trust in God alone for my healing.*

At that time there were only a few of us working together with Mrs. Munroe—Sister Choi and others. I wasn't accustomed to Christian service. Mrs. Munroe would have us in her home on Wong Chuk Street to pray. Mrs. Munroe would kneel to pray for over an hour! I wasn't used to this and considered it very painful. God impressed me to be patient and learn. As a result, I grew spiritually working with her. Now I have been with OMS (Hong Kong Evangelical Church) 42 years.

Finding a marriage partner was something I didn't have faith to believe for, but God provided a good healthy companion for me. God gave us two children, a girl and a boy. I was very happy and satisfied. Rev. Yip Chiu Ming, one of our workers, said, "There are only four of you in this small space. If you have another child, you would qualify for a 200 sq. ft. room in the resettlement estate." So we asked God for another child. Our youngest child is several years younger than his brother.

When I contemplate God's grace to me, I am reminded of a hymn, "Trust and Obey," and also "Wonderful Savior." These two songs have been very helpful to me. All my Christian life, I have relied on God's grace. He has performed many wonderful works. As I have obeyed Him, He has protected me. Therefore, I am very happy! (Yes, Mr. Tang always has a smile and a word of praise to his Savior.)

I remember the reason I gave my last son the name Yiu Chung Kei. There was a government hospital doctor by the name of Cheung Yiu Kei. The school/church where I served asked Dr. Cheung to preach an evangelistic meeting. He was really a powerful preacher. Later I heard him preach with the same anointing to a large rally in the City Hall Auditorium. He earned his living healing people for the government but wouldn't accept money for his preaching ministry of healing souls. As I thought about it, Yiu Kei (glorify Christ), was a great name and so I changed my son's name to Yiu Kei. If he will determine to glorify Christ with his life, that is all I ask. Now Yiu Kei has dedicated his life to God and has entered the seminary to prepare for His service. Praise the Lord!

For many years Mr. Tang has been a good and faithful servant of the Lord, willing to do whatever was asked of him. He is retired, but not really, as he is still helping in the church.

Mary Ellen Beetley, secretary, and bookkeeper for many years. She is helping Mr. Yip Chiu Ming, Principal of one of the rooftop schools.

Rev. Dale McClain teaching and Rev. So interpreting into Cantonese.

CHAPTER 9

A GROWING CHURCH/

REV. TAM WING NIN

The Holy Spirit seemed to be directing in the decision to plan for the opening of a third church, a new ministry center. Where to find this center was not yet clear. God's man was ready, Rev. Tam Wing Nin, one of our young preachers recently graduated from the Hong Kong Bible Institute. (Our OMS Seminary had not yet opened.) After Tam's graduation in the summer of 1958, he helped on the Lei Cheng Uk rooftop in evangelism, played the accordion, led the singing, and sometimes preached. His mother was Mrs. Munroe's housekeeper.

Some years earlier when Mrs. Munroe contacted Mrs. Tam, her son was working in a factory in Hong Kong. The family had come to know the Lord before the Japanese invasion in December 1941, but one by one several of the family members died and Mrs. Tam and her son were left to make their way alone. Wing Nin came to talk with Mrs. Munroe and told her of his early call to preach the Gospel. He tried to ignore it, but it continued to grow in his heart. What should he do? His schooling had been in broken bits. When there was money, he went and when there was none, he tried to study at home. Bible institutes demanded a high school education. He felt too old to go back to high school. Besides, the fees were beyond his means.

With much praying and planning, as well as Mrs. Munroe's help and encouragement, Wing Nin was able to pass the entrance exams, study for four long years, and graduate from the Hong Kong Bible Institute. Another pastor was ready to help shepherd the sheep.

In April 1960, the Hung Hom Chapel opened, pastored by Rev. Tam. This area of Kowloon was industrial and through the years the OMS chapel there, called Yan Chiu Church (Grace Calls or Called by Grace), struggled to stay alive. In later years, after the Tams had emigrated to the United States for ministry with the overseas Chinese, Tam's daughter returned to Hong Kong. An accomplished pianist, she helped with the music in Yan Chiu Church for some time. How wonderful to see how God is continuing to use His servants into the next generation of our early believers.

EARLY CHURCH DEVELOPMENT

In an annual report on Hong Kong OMS Church Development given in January 1963, Dale McClain told that the Every Creature Crusade team moved into town from the New Territories to help two of the churches that were struggling. They were at Yan Yue Church on Boundary Street for three months and moved to Yan Chiu Church, where they launched a campaign from January to April with an initial thrust of 19 consecutive nights of evangelism.

According to Dale's 1963 report, the following describes what the self-support of the churches looked like. *This subject is often naively referred to as the "support of the pastor" economy. A look at our table of statistics shows this to be only one part of the picture. Yan Kwong Tong (First Church), Yan Yue Tong (Second Church), and Yan Chiu Tong (Hung Hom) each involve the monthly financial obligation of three paid workers: number one - pastor; number two - Bible woman; number three - caretaker, plus the rent of the church facility.*

At present First Church is paying 50.2 percent of this total cost; Second Church—42.1 percent; Tai Po Road Church—10 percent; Hung Hom— 11.2 percent. In addition, these churches are paying the current operational costs as well as financing any painting, repairs, plus covering the cost of their annual youth camps and other related ministries.

Self-support prospects *-- not as hopeful as we would wish. We are facing factors of (1) low income bracket memberships, (2) rising rents, (3) the removal of church families from the immediate church area due to government relocation schemes, etc. For the past several years, our first two churches have voted at their annual meetings to increase their monthly giving towards self-support by $50 per month for the succeeding calendar year. At this rate it will require ten more years before our two oldest congregations are fully self-supporting.[14]*

THE HONG KONG EVANGELICAL CHURCH ESTABLISHED/ YAN POON (GRACE ROCK) CHURCH

The third building of the major building project begun by Men For Missions International, Yan Poon Church, was dedicated on Easter Sunday, April 10, 1966. Just days before the dedication service, there had been riots in the streets and Hong Kong was under a curfew for two days and two nights. How thankful we were that the government announced the lifting of the curfew the morning of April 10.

The membership of Grace Rock Church represented the uniting of two of our former churches: Yan Kwong Church at 102 Apliu St. and members of the former Tai Po Street Church, who had been meeting at the rooftop school in Shek Kip Mei. These two congregations moved into the new church on Tong Yam Street in Tai Hang Tung, Kowloon.

Planning for a name for the new combined church included the word for "grace," but what other word would be appropriate? Finally they thought of the word for "rock" because huge boulders had to be broken up and removed from the site before they could build the church. So the name Yan Poon Church, or Grace Rock, was chosen

Here is the real story of the "rock" as told by Mrs. Munroe. She told us this story after the site for the church had been chosen. Maybe this is part of God's way to show us His great knowledge and power and His sense of humor.

Some fifty years ago, I partook in an outdoor picnic with friends in Hong Kong. In those days (1929), Hong Kong and Kowloon were nothing like they are today.

On the Hong Kong side, their first road around the island had just been completed. The cable car and sedan chairs were the only means of transportation to the Peak. On the Kowloon side, there was a chain of villages stretching from the waterfront out toward Lai Chi Kok: Tsim Sha Tsui,

Koon Chung, Yau Ma Tei, Sham Shui Po, etc.
Paddy fields and vegetable gardens lay in between,
and only a narrow trail led to the cemetery.

At that time, my friends and I were living in Yau
Ma Tei. We took a bus toward Sham Shui Po, got off
at about where Boundary Street is today, and walked
across what is now the Tai Hang Tung Recreational
ground to the foot of the mountain. There, in the
shadow of a huge rock that protruded from the side
of the mountain, we decided to eat our picnic lunch.

To add to the gaiety of the occasion, I slipped
away from the others, climbed the mountain to the
top of the rock, walked out on it and sat down. Soon,
someone looked up and saw me. A shout of laughter
went up from them all, and someone snapped a photo
of me. I wish I still had it, but somewhere down
through the years it disappeared.

Three years after this event, I left Hong Kong and
did not return to work there until some 20-plus years
later. By that time, Hong Kong had changed
considerably. The paddy fields and the vegetable
gardens had all vanished, giving place to concrete
buildings full of people. The string of villages had
become one city. Only the mountain and the rock
remained unchanged.

Twenty-five years ago we opened a hall in Sham
Shui Po on Apliu Street, right in the midst of
thousands of people who were living on the streets.
Having fled from China mainland, they had built for
themselves wooden shacks on the mountainside, only
to have them destroyed later by a devastating fire.
Now, they were forced to live in little cubicles on the

sidewalks until better living quarters could be provided for them.

During the week prior to the opening of our gospel hall, Mr. Ho Yui Chi, Miss Choi, Mrs. Law, and I, spent much time each day, praying together. Our equipment was limited to a small organ, a pulpit, and enough chairs to fill the hall. It seemed a great mountain loomed before us, and only with the help of the Lord could we move forward.

As we prayed much, the Holy Spirit directed our attention to the book of Zechariah. In chapter 4, verses 6-10 were especially impressed upon our hearts. Through a study of these verses, we gathered that our success would not be "by might nor by power," but by God's Spirit. By His great grace, the mountain would become a plain. We would not only be able to lay a foundation but would see the finished work. And we were not to "despise the day of small things."

When our hall was finally opened for services, many crowded in to hear, and numbers responded to the claims of the Gospel. We were soon crowded out. Another hall was opened near Boundary Street and it, too, was soon filled.

With the building of the "H" blocks in the resettlement areas, the people were moved from the sidewalks to the large seven-story buildings. It was on the rooftops of these buildings where we began our primary schools. God raised up from among our converts, men and women of every skill, and the work made rapid progress.

As more gospel halls were opened, we began to think of names for them. We had referred to the first two as first and second churches, but to go on with numbers hardly seemed the thing to do. As we discussed the matter, we decided to follow the custom of the Chinese family in naming their children. A first name is chosen for the eldest child, which will belong to every child thereafter. The second name is different, thus distinguishing them from one another. What would we choose for our churches' first name? Someone of our number turned to Zechariah 4:7— "Who art thou, O great mountain? Before Zerubbabel thou shalt become a plain: and he shall bring forth the headstone thereof with shoutings, crying, grace, grace unto it." There was our name— GRACE! Where could we find a better?

Although we now had several halls, still no one of them was large enough to accommodate all the members of that particular church, let alone getting together for a general assembly. We began to pray for an auditorium large enough for this. God heard our prayer and gave us a piece of land. And, strange to say, it lay right at the foot of the mountain, and exactly below the huge rock on which I had sat on that summer day in 1929. In fact, the rock and part of the mountain had to be removed to make room for our church building.

In releasing the contract for the preparation of the ground for building, there was much concern over the rock. How far did it extend back into the mountain? Was it a boulder or was it a protrusion of layers of rock that might be in the mountain? Only excavation would reveal the secret. And it did.

After considerable digging, a huge, round boulder suddenly loosened and came rolling down onto the building site. Now, the workmen had the problem of moving it from the premises. Since it was too large for any equipment to move, it had to be split in pieces. When it had been dynamited apart, they discovered the boulder was of pure granite. The contractors felt amply paid for the efforts they had put forth to loosen the rock, and they presented us with a beautiful piece of granite for the cornerstone of our building.

What shall we call our new church? That was the big question, and we discussed it back and forth. Then someone read Zechariah 4:7, years later, and we all knew we had the answer. It must be Grace Rock.

And here it stands today, a monument of God's faithfulness and of His careful planning over the years. True, there are other buildings and departments that God has added to the work. But Grace Rock Church stands as the foundation, the headstone of them all.[15]

OMS had a center now, with the Chung Yan Primary School, the Kau Yan Medical Center, and Grace Rock Church.[16]

April 12-15, 1966, the OMS-related churches organized into a conference and became known as the Hong Kong Evangelical Church -- HKEC. This was the first annual conference of the local OMS churches. A church administrative committee was chosen, with Field Director Bob Erny as chairman. Later in 1971, when the registration with the government was complete, Rev. Ho was voted as the first chairman of the Hong Kong Evangelical Churches. At that time, we were registered as Hong Kong Evangelical Church (OMS). On March 8, 1985, the name of OMS was legally dropped from the government registration and the church became its own entity. This was in preparation for the handover of Hong Kong back to China in 1997.

Rev. Robert Erny	Field Director
Rev. Grant Nealis	Missionary
Reports	
Evangelism – ECC Team	Rev. Lei Hang On
Church Extension	Rev. Ho Yui Chi
Yan Kwong Church	Rev. Ho Yui Chi
Yan Yue Church	Rev. Peter Law
	Rev. So Tin Wong
Sunday School	Yip Chiu Ming
Yan Din Church & Youth	Tsang Kwong
Yan Chiu Church-Hung Hom	TamWing Nin
Sheung Shui chapel	Yue King Fai
Chuk Yuen – Bamboo Gardens	Hui Mak Lam
Ling Yan (Lei Ching Uk Estate)	Lee Chi Yiu
Chuen Wan Chapel	Tam Nai Chi
Lay Women's report	Mrs. Ho Lin Pui Ying

In the Chairman's report February 26, 1967, for the 13-year anniversary, Ho says:

Since we had the organizing of the local church conference, we have pushed forward. In cooperation,

61

in love, in unity, in economy, we all are facing the positive side. Our church is sending a delegate to Tokyo for the Asian Conference of OMS-related churches this year. Churches and chapels are willing to give money toward the traveling expenses of the delegate. In addition to this, we are also cutting down our subsidies to every church for the coming year. This shows that we are moving forward.

Rev. Ho was chosen as the delegate and on March 26, 1967, he flew to Tokyo for the Asian Conference. He was deeply moved by this trip to Japan and being with the brothers and sisters from all over Asia. Later on in November 1968, Rev. Ho represented the HKEC at the Billy Graham Congress on Evangelism in Singapore.

On the following pages, I have listed all of the churches in the Hong Kong Evangelical church Conference from the beginning of the work of OMS up to the year 1996 including the names of the first pastors.

1954 –1966
Yan Kwong – *Grace Light;* later became Yan Poon- *Grace Rock Church,* Apliu Street in Sham Shui Po – moved to Tong Yam Street in Tai Hang Tung, Mr. Ho Yui Chi, the first pastor we had – continued as the pastor of Grace Church.
1955
Yan Yue – *Showers of Grace;* Tai Po Street in Sham Shui Po, Mr. Peter Law; later Mr. Ng Yue Tong.
1957-1970
Yan Chiu – *Grace Calling;* H Industrial area, Mr. Tam Wing Nin.

1960-1971

Wong Tai Sin Rooftop School, later organized into Yan Shek – *Zion Church,*Wong; Tai Sin Resettlement Village – stayed in the Wong Tai Sin area, Mr. Hui Mak Lam and Rev. Yip Chiu Ming.

1961

Yan Din – *Double Grace;* Kam Tin Village in the New Territories, began by the ECC Team; Mr. Tsang Kwong.

1962

Shueng Shui Chapel – *Upper Waters;* Sheung Shui in the New Territories, near the China border, ECC TEAM – Mr. Yu King Fai, and Mr. Ng Yue Tong.

1964-1967

Chuen Wan Chapel – Bryan Memorial – later organized into Yan Chaak Church – "God's grace pours down on us" – *Streams of Grace;* the industrial town of Chuen Wan in the New Territories, ECC TEAM – Mr. Tam Nai Chi.

1976

Homantin Reading Center – later organized into Yan Kei Church – *Foundation of Grace;* Homantin Resettlement Estate in Kowloon – later moved to Mong Kok District, ECC TEAM – Mr. Joseph Tsang Man Tung. and Rev. Lo Ping Kuen.

1979

Ko Chiu Road Reading Center – Yan Ying Church – *Abundant Grace;* Yau Tong Housing Estate, area beyond Kwun Tong, ECC TEAM – Mr. Alexander Shek Kai Man.

1982

Social Center for the Elderly Yan Fook Church – *Blessing of Grace;* Tai Hing Housing Estate in Tuen Mun, New Territories, Mr. Sunny Chow Ka Shing, with Social Welfare staff.

1983

Tai Yuen Reading Center – Yan Chuen Church – *Perfect & Complete Grace;* Tai Yuen Housing Estate in Tai Po, New territories, Mr. and Mrs. Lo Kwok Keung.

1988

Dragon Garden Church – (The first HKEC mission work) Dragon Garden High Rise Apartment Complex in Macau – 40 miles from HK on the Pearl River Estuary, ECC TEAM – Mr. and Mrs. Tony Kwan.

1991

Choi Yuen Family Service Center – Yan Lam Church – *Grace Raining;* Choi Yuen Housing Estate in Sheung Shui near the HK – China border in the N.T., Mr. Sunny Chow Ka Shing.

1991

Homantin Reading Center – when Yan Kei Church moved to Mong Kok, a daughter church began in the Homantin Reading Center – Yan Ho – *Great Grace;* Homantin Housing Estate – Homantin, Kowloon Yan Kei Church pastor – Rev. Lo Ping Kuen, Mr. Timothy Ho Yiu Wai.

1993`

Wah Ming Family Service Center – Yan Kwong Church – *Grace Light,* Wah Ming Housing Estate – Fanling, N.T., Daughter church of Yan Din Church, Yuen Long, First pastor was Mr. Hung Yan Chuen.

1995

Yan Tin Church – *Fields of Grace;* Baak Tin Housing Estate, Kowloon, daughter church of Grace Rock Church – Mr. Joseph Lai.

1996

Ko Yee Estate Reading Center – Yan Yat Church, *Grace Overflowing;* Ko Yee Housing Estate – Yau Tong, Kowloon, daughter church of Yan Ying Church, first pastor, Mr. Chan Yau Wah.

1996

Home Help Service Center, Tai Ping Housing Estate, Sheung Shui, N.T., daughter church of Yan Lam Church, later joined back to Yan Lam Church.

1996

Yan Yiu Church - *Grace Shining,* Good Rich Garden Complex – Tuen Mun, N.T., second daughter church of Yan Din Church, Yuen Long – Mr. Leung Lin Hing Leon.

Each of these churches has a story all its own. In a later chapter we will share a few of the stories and you will be able to catch some of the wonderful blessings as you read what God has done.

CHAPTER 10

THE EVERY CREATURE CRUSADE

A vitally important ministry of OMS in most countries where we have work is the Every Creature Crusade, "Reaching every person in the nation with a witness for Christ."

In 1960 God led Dale McClain to begin a crusade team in Hong Kong. In March 1961 the Every Creature Crusade (ECC) work began in the village of Kam Tin in the New Territories.

BUDDY GAINES & CHARLES MCNELLY – THE FIRST CRUSADERS

Two young men from the USA, Edgar Henry (Buddy) Gaines III and Charles (Chuck) McNelly, came to Hong Kong to work with a Chinese team in this ministry. Buddy came from South Carolina as a single young man. After three months of language study, Buddy joined the first ECC team. The goal of ECC evangelism was "to reach 'every creature' in the crowded areas of Kowloon and in the New Territories which extend to the China border." The team did some evangelizing for four months in Hung Hom on Cook Street where Rev. Tam was getting the third chapel going. Chuck came from Illinois and, as a young man, had sensed God's hand on him to preach the Gospel of Christ Jesus.

The pattern of the ECC ministry included distributing gospel literature from house to house, preaching in open air meetings, and conducting evening evangelistic services in the rented building where the crusaders lived. Discipleship and training classes were arranged to nurture the new converts. Then a Chinese pastor was appointed to shepherd the little group when it was established as a new congregation of Christian believers.

In the early years of ECC work and ministry in Hong Kong, the distribution of food supplies and clothing was also a necessary part of the outreach. In May 1962 an estimated 75,000 refugees from China crossed into Hong Kong hiding in the mountains, hills, and alleyways until relatives and friends could locate them and give them a safer hiding place. OMS ECC team members carried bags of bread and also shared with them about the One who said: "I am the Bread of Life, whoever eats of Me shall never hunger."

REV. LEI HANG ON – ECC TEAM CAPTAIN

The ECC team captain was Lei Hang On. He had accepted Jesus as his Savior in China when he was about 18 years old. Encouraged by his mother, he studied in the Bible School in Canton that Rev. Munroe began before World War II (see page 10).

Mrs. Lei was studying in the Evangelical Free Church Seminary, also in Canton. They met there and were married in 1943. In 1948 Rev. Lei was pastoring a small church in southern China. The shadow of Communism was spreading further south, and in 1949 the doors to the outside world closed. The Leis suffered many things in the intervening years and finally in 1958, after much prayer, they were given permission to leave China and go to Hong Kong. Rev. Lei remembers, "While we prayed, God gave us a promise: Mark 9:23, 'Everything is possible to him who believes.' On April 28, 1958, we with our five children—the oldest only 13—arrived in Kowloon. We finally found OMS and saw Mrs. Munroe again. She took us in and gave us an opportunity to work in the church. God truly provided a way out for us."

Rev. and Mrs. Lei came to us in the early days of the work in Hong Kong already tempered by suffering. They knew what it meant to trust God for everything.

He began modestly in Hong Kong helping on the first rooftop and preached in the chapel that was held in the OMS office building on Tai Po Road. He was ordained along with Ho Yui Chi, Peter Law, and Tam Wing Nin in March 1963. Then as captain of the ECC team he helped and encouraged the others on the team and led them in door-to-door evangelism. He served with OMS until he retired because of illness. Rev. Lei passed away in 1997. One of the Leis' daughters, Pauline, is married to Rev. Stephen Yik Kai Nin, who has been with OMS for years, teaching in our Taiwan Taichung Bible Seminary.

Buddy and Chuck rotated their times of being in the New Territories and in Kowloon. Buddy recalls some memories of his time in Kam Tin:

This was our first attempt in the ECC ministry for Hong Kong. We experimented and did our best. Every morning and afternoon our teams would go out to the homes, walled villages, and out in the paddy fields sharing the Gospel of Jesus Christ. In the evenings we conducted evangelistic meetings in the same house where we slept on the second floor. The team members were Mr. Lei Hang On, Mr. Peter Au, Mr. Fong, Mr. Choi, Mr. Tang, and the team cook. During my time there we also ministered in the village of Shek Wu Tong. This was out in the paddy fields near Kam Tin.

After the chapel in Kam Tin was going well, and the Tsang family was settled in the work, the ECC team moved on to the village of Sheung Shui. This village was just a stone's throw from the Hong Kong-China border. In some places it was easy to see the mountains that were in China. The team stayed there until the gospel hall was established. Mr. Ng Yue Tong was the team member who remained behind to continue the ministry begun there. During that year of ministry some amazing statistics were recorded. These show the work of the ECC team and more important, the work of the Holy Spirit. The following numbers tell some of the story:

- *41,266 homes visited*
- *634 follow-up visits*
- *427 total number of decisions in homes and services*
- *74 response by mail*

The beginning of the work in Sheung Shui was very encouraging, but as time went along it did not continue strong. The work was hard and although a preaching point was established, it only continued for a few years. There were just not enough people to support a pastor and the needs of the church. In 1971, the chapel in Sheung Shui was closed. The ECC team moved into the city to help the city churches with their evangelistic work.

When Buddy finished his 27 months with OMS and the ECC team, he was loaned to World Vision to help in Macau. During his 15 months there, he began the Timothy Institute for destitute Chinese children. This was a wonderful work and many children found love and the Lord Jesus as their Savior. Buddy returned to the United States in March 1964.

Chuck finished his time with OMS and the ECC team but continued to work in Hong Kong for many years and founded a home for street kids. He exhibited his love for the Chinese youth in very practical ways and helped many come to know the Lord Jesus Christ.

REV. & MRS. TSANG KWONG – PASTOR FIRST ECC CHURCH

Towards the end of the time, the ECC team was in Kam Tin, a very rural area with rice paddies and water buffalo. Rev.Tsang Kwong and his wife joined the team with the plan to continue there as the pastor. Kam Tin Village has a unique and interesting history. It is two walled villages close together. Only one remains intact and it is now a tourist attraction representing life around 800 years ago. The following information comes from a plaque on the outside of the wall beside the gate:

"Kat Hing Wai" -- All the inhabitants of this "Wai" or walled village, have the surname "Tang." Their ancestors who moved from Central and Southern China during a period of unrest were among the first to populate this area. In the 13th century, the Tang family gave shelter to the last of the Sung ruling dynasty and one Tang married an aunt of the Emperor. The sons of this marriage are the founders of various clans in the neighboring rural area. When China leased the New Territories in 1898, this village was closed to the entry of the British Forces. The wrought iron gates of this, the only entrance, were confiscated. In 1925, the gates were ceremonially restored as a token of goodwill. The gates had been discovered in Ireland. Today the villagers cultivate the surrounding rice and vegetable fields. Their village with wall and moat stands as an unspoiled example of a typical Cantonese community, insulated against the banditry prevalent some two hundred years ago.

When the Every Creature Crusade team found the little house to rent, it happened to be close to the wall of the other village across the road. Bob Erny talks about "The House by the Wall" in an article in the June 1970 *Missionary Standard*:

There is in the village of Kam Tin a small house. Lying close to the thick shadow of the "Tai Hung Wai" wall, the gloom of that 500-year-old bulwark seemed to have settled upon it. Centuries of superstition and ignorance had

*made the hoary walls more than a physical
barrier. The Tang clan, inhabitants of the
ghetto-like enclosure, long had their private
taboos as well as their clannish pride. "No man
from our settlement," they had been heard to
boast, "has ever joined that foreign religion."*

Then the Tsangs arrived. They were a warm
outgoing family with five youngsters and they spoke with
the same Hakka dialect as the villagers. When Mrs. Tsang
announced she was opening a kindergarten in her house
and invited the villagers to send their children, it seemed
quite natural to do so. With the Tsangs around, that
"foreign religion" didn't seem foreign at all. The Tsang
family themselves had not always known the foreigner's
God.

In Mrs. Tsang's testimony, told to me in May 1988,
she says:

*I was born into a family that worshiped idols.
My parents were quite wealthy and were
landowners. My sisters and I went to school in
Canton, where we lived. After I married, my
husband became an officer in the Nationalist Army
of China and our life was good. Then the worst
happened and the Communists came. Because I
was a landowner's daughter and landowners were
suffering, and because my husband was a
Nationalist Army officer, we felt it imperative to
flee to Hong Kong. This was 1950. After arriving
we didn't know how to make a living. We had*

*taken money with us so we had enough for awhile.
Actually we weren't willing to work, as we didn't
see anything suitable for us. Some things were too
high and we couldn't reach to them; some jobs
were low and we didn't want to do them. My
husband was an officer, you see! So neither of us
did anything.*

Several years passed and all their money was gone.
With six children and Mrs. Tsang's elderly mother with them,
they needed something to keep them alive. Mrs. Tsang tells
that she was so depressed and even thought of death. But her
sister-in-law had heard of Jesus and talked to her.

*My sister-in-law came again and told me to
believe in Jesus because He would help me. So I
went with her to hear about Jesus. That night the
evangelist spoke from Matthew 6:25. He said, "Do
not worry about your life." I listened very carefully
because I was worrying about my life. Why
shouldn't one worry about his life? That night God
spoke through the evangelist using Matthew 6:25-34,
especially verse 33-- "Seek first the kingdom of God
and His righteousness and all these things will be
given to you as well." My heart was happy because
when I was so poor and heartbroken, Jesus came to
save me. In my deep need no one came to help me,
no friend or relative, but I found that Jesus loved me.*

*I kept going to the meetings and wanted my
husband to go. He was quite a stubborn man and
didn't want to go. He couldn't understand why I was*

so happy, so one night he finally went with me. In 1955 we were both believers and prayer became a part of our lives after that.

It was strange to think that before we put our trust in Jesus, we weren't willing to do any work. Then when we thought how Jesus left heaven and His glory to come to earth to save us, why weren't we willing to use our hands in labor? Oh, how we changed after we believed in the Lord Jesus.

Eventually Mrs. Munroe noticed the keenness and eagerness of this couple and asked them if they would teach in the rooftop school. God heard the prayers of the Tsangs and they began to be in leadership positions. Mr. Tsang felt that he didn't know the Bible well enough, so when OMS opened the seminary, Mr. Tsang applied to study. He graduated after a few years. It was then that the Tsangs were asked to go to Kam Tin where the ECC team had been working.

Mrs. Tsang talks about her children:

My children learned early to love Jesus. When I gave them money for food, they didn't want to spend it but put it in the offering for Jesus. Living in the village meant that the school fees were less expensive and the children were able to study. They had asked Jesus into their hearts and had learned to obey. Several of them earned high enough marks that the school fees were waived. It seemed that they really understood a lot of the meaning from God's Word because they knew they should be diligent. When they were small, we gave them

HK$0.10 for their offering in Sunday school and taught them about the tithe to God. I praise the Lord for the children's obedience and that from small to big, they have been taught the importance of giving to God.

The legacy left by Rev. and Mrs. Tsang is that every one of their children is walking with the Lord and their oldest son, David Tsang Chiu Sui, is also a minister of the Gospel of Christ.

The work in Kam Tin grew, fueled by the love and dedication of the Tsang family. For a while they had a preaching point in Shek Woo Tong, just near to the Kam Tin Village. When the ministry grew and the little house where the church met couldn't hold the people, they considered where they should go.

By then, Rev. Tsang had been ordained and in 1965, the church had become an organized church. It became Yan Din Church, or Double Grace Church. It was the fourth of the churches to take a name with Grace in it. When Rev. Tsang finally retired in his 70's, his son David was ready to take over the church as its pastor. The elder Rev. Tsang went to heaven and rested in the Lord's bosom (Chinese translation) on August 10, 1982.

David Tsang studied in seminary in Hong Kong and later at Asbury Seminary in the States. David and his family moved the church to the nearby growing town of Yuen Long. So many of the young people had left the villages for work in the towns, and by moving to Yuen Long, David hoped to reach out to more of the young people and couples. The church became one of the largest churches of the Hong Kong Evangelical Church and many young people have found the

Lord there. Perhaps it should be mentioned here that moving the church didn't mean that they had a church building that was larger. What it meant for the Yan Din Church was the purchasing of two apartments on the second floor of a high-rise building. They remodeled the apartments to be used for worship and multi-purpose for meetings, Sunday school, and fellowship. The Hong Kong concept of church is just a bit different than we think of church here in America. Most of the churches are found in high-rise buildings on the second or third floors in purchased or rented apartments or flats, as they are called in Hong Kong.

Yan Din Church continues to expand and grow under the leadership of Rev. and Mrs. Christopher Pang. They have purchased a third small apartment on the same floor and are praying that the Lord will make a way for them to own the entire first floor of the high-rise building. In 1998 they averaged 199 people every Sunday for church and the space for worship is filled to the maximum. A letter from Mrs. Pang in October 1999 says that they have more than 200 per Sunday. Now they are considering two services on Sunday, unusual in the HK churches, or they may have to find a larger place. This would be costly. Many young people and young couples are members, and it is a joy to see them growing in the Lord.

Psalm 118 begins and ends with "Give thanks to the Lord, for he is good; his love endures forever." Why is it hard to open our lips and give praise and thanks to the Lord? One of my experiences while working in the Yan Din Church showed the hearts of two very poor women who could thank God in every circumstance, and I thank God for their witness to me and my memories of them.

Some of the elderly had come to know Jesus during the time the church was located in Kam Tin Village. They could walk or ride a mini-bus with little trouble. When the church moved to the city, it was harder for some to come unless others helped them. On my Fridays at the church, some of the young people took me to the little homes in the village and helped me with translation and Bible reading. We had visited Auntie Hing before and my thought was that most people had garages that were lovely compared to her shack. Her hut was built on a lean-to at the very end of the old brick houses in the village. Beyond was a ditch and lots of tropical vegetation. Just remembering it gives me the creeps, which describes what would crawl across her cement floor.

On this visit we took the cassette player, a sermon tape, and our Bibles. We had a little worship service with Auntie Hing. After Robson had explained the sermon a little more clearly to her, she got off her wooden bed down onto her knees on the cement floor. We thought she wanted to look for something, but she folded her hands and began to pray. She prayed for us and thanked the Lord that we had come to visit. Then she began thanking the Lord for a whole list of things, not the least of which was being thankful that Jesus helps her cook her rice and take care of herself. Then she got up and sat down on her typical hard bed with the mosquito netting hanging down. I forgot to mention one thing! *Auntie Hing is completely blind.* What a humbling experience. In the sermon tape were two verses that are great!

• *But as for you, be strong and do not give up, for your work will be rewarded* (2 Chronicles 15:7).

• *For the eyes of the Lord range throughout the earth to strengthen those whose hearts are fully committed to him* (2 Chronicles 16:9a).

Another time when we were there, it was raining and the water just flowed across her floor from one side to the other. Still she would get up, light the kerosene hot plate, and cook her food. Eventually, the church people helped her move into the city to the Center for the Blind where she had a room and help.

The other lady was my friend, Chan Kwai Chee, whom I have talked about in my letters. The first time I met her was with some of the young people who took me out along the rice fields and duck farms. We walked down village paths past small shrines to the earth god. At one place there was a huge old banyan tree with "god shelves" and lots of candles and incense under its huge spreading branches. Certain trees were worshiped by many of the animistic villagers. On we walked along the paths and finally came to Kwai Chee's place beside a fishpond. Can you imagine the size of the mosquitoes that bred in that water? Her hut was owned by a nearby neighbor who had used the hut for pigs. Yes, pigs!! They had cleaned it out and Kwai Chee lived there in rather primitive conditions with an outhouse and shower built in a little lean-to just outside her door. She had the ubiquitous mosquito net over her cot because those critters were big! This old lady with a sunny disposition, a big almost toothless smile, and a thankful heart welcomed us into her "home."

Before I left Hong Kong, Kwai Chee was very weak and not well. Again her church family stepped in to help and found a space for her in the Kam Tin Home for the Elderly. She lived in a corner of a room with four other old ladies. All she had was a bed, a bedside table, a big Chinese padded quilt, and she added, "a roof over my head, food to eat, and people to help me." She thanked God for all and continued to put her trust in Him as a child would. Her faith was so childlike. She was an uneducated woman, who had lost all her family in China and found her way to Hong Kong. I saw my dear friend again in February 1999, and at the age of 95 she still remembered me. In a letter from the pastor's wife, she told me that Kwai Chee had died in her sleep on October 10, 1999. Her simple faith in her Jesus never wavered. I thank God for these dear ones who have ministered to me by their lives. Their light still shines for you to see the way.

Yan Din Church began a daughter church in a new housing area in Fanling, New Territories. Twenty-one members from Yan Din Church went to be the nucleus of the new church. The HKEC Conference applied to the government for this family center. In every new housing district the government decides on the social services that should be in that area—for example, reading study rooms, kindergartens, centers for the elderly, family centers, youth centers, etc. Different organizations apply for these various service centers, so no one is guaranteed that they will get what they applied for. This has been one of the creative ways that the church in Hong Kong has been able to grow since buying land is not possible. Only those organizations that were granted land in the early days of development now have ground on which to build. To have ground to build a church, an organization must also supply some social service to the community, such as a school.

Recently, Yan Din Church began a second daughter church in another new housing development in Tuen Mun (this used to be Castle Peak). This new church is entirely the project of the Yan Din Church people with no help from the HKEC Conference. The work begun in 1954 by the OMS missionaries has come full circle.

"Buddy" Edgar H. Gaines III, one of the first two missionaries who came to HK to work with the ECC team

Billy Campbell, Crusader with the ECC team. Eating is a favorite pasttime!!!

The first Crusade workers and evangelistic team with Mrs. Munroe.

An outdoor meeting in an old village in the New Territories

ECC members carried bags of bread, which they gave along with the Gospel, to the thousands of weary and hungry refugees who escaped across the China-Hong Kong border to freedom.

Rev. Tsang, pastor of the first Every Creature Crusade Church

Rev. Lee Hang On, Rev. Law, Rev. Ho and Rev. Dale McClain looking at a map of Hong Kong's New Territories, planning where the ECC team should begin their work.

Dorothy visiting her good friend, Chan Kwai Chi, in 1977.

CHAPTER 11

MORE MISSIONARIES JOIN THE HONG KONG FAMILY – GRANT & DOTTIE NEALIS
1961-1983

Grant and Dottie Nealis and baby Jonathan left San Francisco harbor on January 21, 1961, bound for Hong Kong. Before their marriage, Grant spent two years in the OMS Every Creature Crusade work in Japan and Dottie spent a year in Brazil teaching the missionaries' children. On February 11, 1961, their ship docked at the Kowloon pier. While they waited to be cleared by Hong Kong Immigration, they stood at the rail of the ship talking to the missionaries down on the pier—Dale and Polly McClain, Bob and Phyllis Erny, Auntie Mun, and Buddy Gaines. Those were the days folks traveled by ship. Grant remembers their first impression of the Hong Kong weather in February as being cold and damp. They didn't see the sun for six weeks and had a hard time getting warm—no central heating, fireplaces, or stoves, and only kerosene heaters that smoked!

Since Grant and Dottie also went to the language school in the Hong Kong University on Hong Kong Island, they followed much the same methods of transportation as the Ernys when they went to language school. A car ride, two buses, and a ferry ride brought them to their destination – an hour one way. Grant said when he was energetic, he used the travel time to learn the Chinese characters on flash cards. Yes, we all understand John Nealis was only eight months old when they arrived in Hong Kong, but in the years that followed three lovely girls joined the family, all made in Hong Kong! Nancy Rose was first, and then came Melody Ruth and Cherry Sue. Today these children all have families of their own and are all walking with the Lord.

RON & PRISCILLA HARRINGTON
1962-1966

Ron Harrington, a businessman, was asked to go to Hong Kong to be the director of the building program and the business manager. He and his wife, Priscilla, went to Hong Kong in 1961 to be introduced to those involved in the building project and see what he would be doing. Then in August 1962 the Harringtons arrived and jumped immediately into the work.

Ron and Priscilla and their two children, Roy and Sylvia, were a welcome addition to the missionary family. The children were already in their teens, so Roy went to high school in Taiwan and Sylvia studied for a year in the British system. That was a difficult time for her and the next year she joined her brother in Taichung, Taiwan, studying at Morrison Academy.

Priscilla was a wonderful field hostess. She said, "There was a nine-month stretch without a vacant guest bed or an extra place at the table." She had a young Chinese girl helping her, one who had fled China with family left behind. Many guests came in those early days because Hong Kong was billed as "a shoppers paradise." Visitors and friends saw what God was doing in this small bit of land that overflowed with people. Priscilla also taught an English Bible class in the Hung Hom (Yan Chiu) –1996 Chapel and on one of the rooftops.

DUANE BEALS AND DOROTHY BACKER
1963-1996

Duane Beals from Indiana arrived in Hong Kong, September 10, 1963, to begin his ministry with the Every Creature Crusade. I arrived September 26, a nurse from Oregon. Soon both Duane and I were very involved in language study. We began at the new Yale-In-China program that had come to Hong Kong the year before. Priscilla was the first one to study in this program. We didn't have to cross the harbor to Hong Kong Island, but via bus we found our way to the study center in Kowloon. You didn't need to be polite getting on a bus in those days for two reasons: (1) You would never be able to get on the bus, and (2) You would be late for language school. After being late a couple of times and watching people, even polite-looking Chinese gentlemen, elbow their way onto the bus, I decided to follow suit. It was an experience only for sardines. I am thankful that later on, when people *queued* (British for lined up) between steel barriers, boarding a bus was no longer very exciting. After two years of language study, I took up responsibilities in the new clinic that had been built.

At the time we arrived in 1963, Hong Kong had not had rain for some months and drought had caused much suffering and hardship for the people. In Rev. Ho's quarterly report, he said:

The hot, sultry weather is upon us here in Hong Kong and it seems to be hotter than years before. According to the report, this May is unprecedented during this century. It has not rained for several months. The hot sun is like a fire umbrella above us. The ground cracks and the grains dry. The bottom of the reservoirs in Hong Kong can be seen and the weeds are growing. Now we have water only once in every four days and it is at a dangerous stage. Because of the shortage of water, it affects our living problems. It is a great hardship to trade and to the farmers. Every religion, such as Catholics, Buddhists and Taoists, are praying for rain. Our members also have had a prayer meeting to especially pray for rain. First we prayed that God would take pity on the Hong Kong people, that they might understand God's will and ask Him to forgive their sins, for they have been praying to the idols instead of the true God. We prayed that God would give us plenty of rain in accordance with His will. We are united in prayer for this purpose.

Would you be thankful for eight hours of water a day? You would be when it has been restricted for almost a year. In June 1964, Rev. Ho's report said, "Our merciful God looks after the people in Hong Kong. He has given us much rain. Our water supply is not restricted anymore. We have eight hours of water every day."

How well I remember those days. It was a time of learning to trust the Lord and also learning a different lifestyle. We had four hours of water every fourth day.

During that time all available containers were refilled with water. All the jobs that required more water had to be done quickly. Water was too precious to waste in those days. Washing all clothes by hand was something I thought only the pioneers did. Well, we did it, too, because we did not have a washing machine. Try washing a bed sheet by hand and then hanging it out the window clipped to a long bamboo pole for drying. It was like holding on to a huge unwieldy flag flying in the wind. What an experience! All this was accomplished between 6 a.m. and 8:30 a.m. when we had to be heading out the door to catch a bus to language school.

Actual finished buildings—First completed was Chung Yan Primary School, "Praise Grace." In the middle is Kau Yan Medical Center, "Saving Grace." Left the church is called Yan Poon, "Grace Rock."

Ron Harrington and Florence Munroe in front and Dale McClain behind with two men from the Government's Registrars Office – August 1962.

Preparing to lay the foundation stone for the new OMS primary school with the missionary team present. Left to Right: Polly McClain, Dottie Nealis, Priscilla Harrington, Dick and Doug McClain kneeling in front, Mary Ellen Beetley, Mrs. Florence Munroe, Carol McClain, in back: Grant Nealis, Ron Harrington, Dr. Stanley Tam, Dale McClain.

CHAPTER 12

STORY OF A VISION

In Hong Kong over half the population were young people under the age of 15. Thousands had no place to go to school and, as children of refugee families, they often could not attend school because there was no money. In those days tuition was charged in all schools. With so many children to evangelize and educate and so small a place in which to work, OMS needed room to expand.

A vision was born. As early as 1957 OMS had approached the British government for a grant of land. Months and years of praying and waiting passed before we were advised that land would be granted for a school and medical center. An adjacent parcel could be purchased for a center for evangelism. In June 1959 the Hong Kong government presented this project to OMS. The government needed more people to help with the refugees flooding Hong Kong. Even after 1949 people continued to come from China through many dangers and trials. They searched for freedom from oppression and relief from hunger and starvation.

The property granted to OMS was in the midst of refugee shacks and adjoining the seven-story resettlement buildings with some 40,000 residents. This was in Tai Hang Tung area, (Big East Ditch), where OMS already had a rooftop school.

With the obvious increase in population and all the churches in rented quarters, OMS felt the urgent need for a central working base. In August 1962 the Hong Kong government approved a 25,828 square-foot land grant to

OMS. This included 19,364 square feet, a free grant for a school and clinic and 6,464 square feet for building a church to be paid for by OMS.[17] Bob Erny commented in the February 1966 *Missionary Standard* that the land from the Hong Kong government was priced at US$7.00 per square foot. With surety, God granted us a miracle.

In the October 1959 *Missionary Standard*, Dr. Eugene Erny, president of OMS, stated that Prayer Circle groups had joined with Men For Missions councils, feeling God had placed the challenge of raising money for the OMS Hong Kong project before them. With faith and enthusiasm they undertook raising the necessary $75,000 for the project.

In the June 1963 *Missionary Standard*, an article by project building supervisor Ron Harrington told about Dale McClain sharing the vision of the building project at the Men For Missions Rally at Winona Lake, Indiana, in July 1961. Ron added, "Men For Missions International and The Oriental Missionary Society will be forever grateful to World Vision, Inc., and Dr. Bob Pierce for assuming a large share of the financial responsibility for the medical center."

The land grants could not be completed until official notification had been received from the Hong Kong government. Ron said, "At long last, the day came on August 14, 1962. Auntie Mun, Dale McClain, and I went to the office of the government registrar. Auntie Mun, acting on behalf of The Oriental Missionary Society, executed the leases with the Crown for the land grants. God had enabled us to move another step nearer the fulfillment of the vision."

Do you remember in the Old Testament how God gave Joseph favor with those government officials and he was able to be God's witness? So Ron was able to do the same thing with all the people coming and going related to the building project.

1963 saw many new things happening. On February 16, the long-awaited groundbreaking took place for the Hong Kong building project. Then in March we joyfully witnessed four of our co-workers receive their ordination: Ho Yui Chi, Lei Hang On, Peter Law, and Tam Wing Nin. Each one of these men came to this place of responsibility, joy, and service knowing what sorrow and suffering meant.

Another huge milestone was passed when on July 31 the foundation stone for the new OMS Christian Primary School was laid. Stanley Tam, an American businessman and OMS board member, arrived early on the evening of July 30. Florence Munroe, just winding up her New Zealand-Australian tour, arrived later the same evening. The Lord had timed all details right to the hour. The P.A. equipment was set up with plenty of volume, for the ceremony took place amidst the clang and din of construction work. We were working hard to meet the deadline for the opening of school in September. The block and tackle lowered the stone firmly into place. Stanley poured the cement. We had passed another milestone in this long construction program—all to the glory of God!

NEW PRIMARY SCHOOL OPENS

In December 1963 Dr. and Mrs. Paul Petticord were speakers for the united service. All the churches gathered on the ground floor open play area of the primary school to praise the Lord for the finished construction of Chung Yan Primary School. Dr. Petticord was president of Western

Evangelical Seminary in Portland, Oregon, and chairman of the OMS Board of Directors.

More than 600 children were enrolled at the beginning of school. The government estimated that it takes 30 months for a new school to reach full capacity. Our capacity would be about 1,000 students. (Remember, you don't begin with a full crop of fourth, fifth, and sixth graders. You must "grow" your own!) At the writing of this article for the January 1965 *Missionary Standard*, only 11 months had gone by since school opened. To have a student body with more than 600 was a real success. This new school began to be self-supporting, operating with a black balance every month.

It was fitting that the name of the school should be Chung Yan School, which means "Praise Grace." During the years of this primary school, many children were introduced to the Lord Jesus Christ. Amazing as it seems, Bible could be taught in all schools.

Dr. and Mrs. Paul Petticord, Chairman of the OMS Board, received a huge welcome from the students of Chung Yan.

CHAPTER 13

ECC TEAM IN CHUEN WAN

In January 1964 the Every Creature Crusade began ministering in the strategic industrial location of Chuen Wan. Grant Nealis worked with the ECC team after language school and had to prepare sermons in Chinese to preach in the new chapels—not an easy task! Early in their missionary career, Dottie's father passed away quite suddenly. They were not able to return home for his funeral, but a wonderful memorial was later set up in his memory. There was a great response to the Gospel message and a growing congregation was born through the work of the ECC team in Chuen Wan. Hong Kong was crowded with refugees, and the demand for space far exceeded the supply. Rent was extremely high. The hall in Chuen Wan was purchased with the help of many Christians overseas and as a memorial to Dottie's parents, Mr. and Mrs. T. M. Bryan, who lived in Memphis, Tennessee, and had been vitally interested in the work of the church.[18]

After Duane Beals finished his three months of language study, he moved to Chuen Wan to live with the ECC team and learn from them as he witnessed their lives of fun and dedication to the Lord. The Chuen Wan Gospel Chapel was dedicated on November 13, 1964, to the glory of God.

During the time that the ECC team was in Chuen Wan, Rev. Joe Rogers, OMS Northwest regional director, came and spent some time with us in Hong Kong. He went out and lived with the team for a couple of nights. Joe found out that the team members were not all about seriousness but loved fun and foolishness. He had quite a shock when a string of firecrackers went off under his cot. Still in his sleeping bag, he flew off that cot into a corner, shouting that the soldiers were coming. (Those were the days when firecrackers were still legal in Hong Kong.) Yes, the men loved fun, and how they loved the Lord!

Duane not only had a good ministry with the Crusade team, but he also filled in for a time as our business manager and spent a couple of months in Australia and New Zealand sharing about the ministry and needs of Hong Kong. In 1966 Duane's fiancee, Charlotte Burelison, came to Hong Kong and they were married in April in the Chinese Christian and Missionary Alliance Church. (Our OMS church was not yet registered with the government to perform weddings.) Duane and Charlotte returned to the States where their two daughters, Susan and JoLynn, were born. Duane has pastored and has also spent many years training young men and women for the ministry. He is presently on the staff at Bethel College in Indiana and serves on the OMS Board of Directors.

REV. TAM NAI CHI - ECC TEAM MEMBER
1963-1971

Tam Nai Chi was a young man who had originally joined the ECC team when they went to Kam Tin. To gain more Bible training, Mr. Tam enrolled in our new seminary, juggling study and ministry with the ECC team in Kam Tin.

He began working on Shek Kip Mei rooftop in early 1963, studying at the seminary each morning. After combining his study and work, he finally finished his three-year course. In the fall, after graduation, he was back with the Every Creature Crusade team. He helped as the team entered Chuen Wan with the goal to visit every family and share the good news of Jesus Christ. After the ECC team left, Rev. Tam and his wife stayed to pastor this budding church.

On April 2, 1967, the congregation of the Chuen Wan chapel was established into an organized church with about 30 members, and the church was growing. The name they chose was "Yan Chaak" which means grace and light or water. Rev. Tam said, "To speak more fully, it means the grace of God pours down like a flood upon us."

He talked about the problems of May 1967, when the Red Guards from China tried to come into Hong Kong and the local Communists stirred up trouble. They brought fear, riots, and disorder; prices of food escalated and businesses were in a state of depression. Rev. Tam's September 1967 report says:

> *Many thanks for your intercession on our behalf that we might live in peace and safety during the time of unrest in Hong Kong. I think of God's promise, "In me ye might have peace. In the world ye have tribulation, but be of good cheer, I have overcome the world." We know the more we have tribulation, the more we should depend on God. So during these several months we have overcome all difficulties in spite of the terrorism and high prices of food. You probably have heard about the trouble*

in Hong Kong, but I feel Hong Kong is not in danger but in safety.

I remember coming back to Kowloon from Hong Kong Island on the Star Ferry with my brother, David, who was on R&R from Vietnam. When we reached the Kowloon side, the bus terminus by the ferry terminal was crowded with angry men putting big posters on the back of the buses, which were going nowhere. We could feel the angry tension in the air. All I wanted to do was to get away from there as quickly as possible before any attention could be directed at us, the foreigners. It was a very scary moment.

Several times during the years, Rev. Tam experienced serious illnesses and was hospitalized for surgery. In February 1971 he missed the Annual Conference meeting because he was in the hospital. He was there about a week. Finally, on October 26, 1971, the Lord took Rev. Tam home to heaven, after suffering with liver cancer.

After Rev. Tam passed away, the church struggled and the attendance dwindled. The original location of the church, which was so promising at the beginning because people passed to and fro through the square, now became an obscure place. Businesses changed and the square was no longer a place where many people passed by.

In the late '70s a young man fresh out of seminary and full of enthusiasm was asked to take on the challenge of Yan Chaak Church. He did a wonderful job as they moved the church to a more suitable location, and with more room they began to grow. Somewhere along the way disunity crept in, and after awhile the young man who had lifted the church out of the doldrums left Yan Chaak, taking a great part of the congregation with him. Right down to the present time, the church continues to struggle. A number of different ones have led the church for a while, but the work in that area is difficult, and the church continues to struggle.

Skipping over some years into the early 90's, a young pastor came to the Hong Kong Evangelical Church and was asked to take charge of Yan Chaak Church. Sammy Cheng has a story that most of us cannot relate to, but his testimony brings glory to the Lord Jesus Christ and the ministry of the Holy Spirit in a life turned over to Him.

Born into a poor refugee family, Sammy found daily existence extremely difficult. His father left when Sammy was ten and died two years later. One of six children, he was often on his own while his mother worked long hours to feed her family. Like most of his friends and neighbors, Sammy didn't know how to do much, except get into trouble. He finally put in the required school time and made it through the 11th grade. Gambling, fighting, and hanging out became his daily life and at age 13 he joined a Triad gang. (Triads are Chinese secret societies generally involved in criminal activities, a Chinese equivalent to the Mafia.) When asked to join gang fights or carry out illegal activities, he willingly complied, eager to prove himself to those who seemingly cared about him. Enmeshed in the Triad brotherhood, he became increasingly estranged from his natural family.

As a young adult, with no purpose or plan in life, Sammy slept all day and fought at night. Several times he tried to quit this lifestyle, but found life boring and dull. The money he earned was not nearly enough for the lifestyle he desired. The Triad brotherhood came to his aid, setting him up as a drug dealer and moneylender.

At first he was strong, selling the drugs only to others. Since his older brother was an addict, Sammy had vowed to avoid that trap. But as the months passed and the fulfillment dimmed, Sammy forgot his pledge. In swift and powerful addiction he lost everything. A profound sense of worthlessness consumed him.

At this point of desperation, Sammy met a recovering drug addict who told him about a Gospel Drug Treatment Center. Although he had never heard of such a place, he was desperate enough to try anything. At the meetings he didn't understand and didn't care about all the religious talk. But he stayed, hoping to be freed of drugs. There he met other former addicts—sincere, friendly men who treated him with kindness and respect. Envying their strong, healthy bodies and wanting to be like them, he agreed to enter the rehabilitation camp.

The first days and weeks of withdrawal were a nightmare, but his new brothers stayed beside him. In humility and love they prayed for him, read from the Word of God, and cheered his victories. Although his body was in turmoil, a sense of inner peace gave hope that this time he could make it. For almost a year Sammy lived in the camp on a secluded beach far from the city. Long days of hard labor brought physical restoration and strength.

As his body healed, so did his heart. In daily chapel services he heard about Someone who loved him completely—Someone willing to forgive him. One night, alone on the beach, Sammy accepted Jesus as his new master—a master powerful enough to salvage hopeless addicts.

Upon completion of his recovery program, Sammy decided to remain in the camp and help others. For two years

God used him to restore and share the Good News with other men caught in sin's trap. As his faith matured, his desire to love, serve, and know God more fully deepened. He yearned to be a preacher of the Gospel. It seemed an impossible dream. Although uncertain it could happen, he dedicated himself to serving God full time. For further training he entered seminary and met the young Christian lady who became his wife.

Sammy's dream came true as he pastored a church of his own here in Hong Kong. From the ashes of despair, God molded a man of humility, joy, and servanthood—a man determined to share hope and life with a dying world.[19]

Why are we surprised when God lifts a man from a powerful drug addiction and calls him to preach the Gospel?

Look at the amount of rice the Crusade Team eats—Rev. Lee Hang On, Mr Yau, Tam Nai Chi and the boy helper.

Dorothy Backer and Duane Beals soon to leave for Hong Kong—
Our display at Winona Lake, Indiana OMS Conference in 1963.
(A refugee shack!)

Harry and Eleanor Burr, President of Men For Missions, came to lay
the foundation stone for the Medical Center.

CHAPTER 14

TRANSITIONS

A special service was held March 1, 1964, and the new Chung Yan Primary School was dedicated to the Lord. There was room for 1,000 students in morning and afternoon sessions. During those first ten years, people were added to the church and more men and women were trained in the OMS Bible Seminary. In May 1964 three young men graduated. Peter Au helped as translator for the missionary on the ECC team. Tam Nai Chi was ordained and pastored the Chuen Wan Church "Yan Chaak," and Yue Ka Lei pursued a teaching career. He has faithfully served in the Grace Rock Church for many years as a deacon and in other roles.

FLORENCE MUNROE LEAVES HONG KONG
Summer 1964

Later in the summer Florence Munroe left Hong Kong for good, having reached retirement age. It is always hard to see one era come to an end, but the joys of those who found Jesus as Savior during Auntie Mun's years of ministry will never end. Mrs. Munroe did not retire, but went to South America and Ecuador to work among the many Cantonese-speaking Chinese who had emigrated there. One of her helpers there was Doris Mak who later became our Chinese secretary and bookkeeper in Hong Kong. After she emigrated to the United States, Doris worked for some years as a cashier at OMS Headquarters in Greenwood, Indiana.

Mrs. Munroe went to Australia for several years and ministered to the Cantonese-speaking Chinese living there. This paraphrase of Psalm 23 is from Sidney Wong, a friend:

> *The Lord is my shepherd, I never lack because of his inexhaustible supply. He lets me rest on a green lawn where my spirit can get full. He guides me to a peaceful stream when I am thirsty and tired. When I am weak in faith, he restores my soul. Then he guides me in the right, safe, and straight way, and doesn't let me get lost. Although I had been through a calamity and passed a death valley, yet I am not frightened, because the Shepherd is with me. He protects me with his stick and pole. Meanwhile, he lets me know that he loves me. All this makes me get great consolation. He displays good things on a table for me, and these right before my enemy's eyes. He plasters me with the oil of rejoicing and makes my face smooth and my heart full of his happy tidings. All of my life is by the grace of God. I want to live in the palace of God forever.*

Goodbyes are a part of the life of a missionary, but they are never easy. In the spring of 1965, Dale and Polly McClain and their children returned to the USA for a homeland assignment as well as getting their oldest child, Carol, ready for college. They represented Hong Kong at the OMS Conference at Winona Lake, Indiana, that year.

In preparation for his leaving the field, Dale turned over the field leadership to Bob Erny, who had been appointed field director by the OMS Board. He carried that responsibility for several years through some exciting times of growth and maturation of our Chinese church.

Dr. Charles Omdal, Dorothy Backer and Phyllis Erny, nurses, and Mr. Henry Allen of the Refugee Authority. They helped us get equipment.

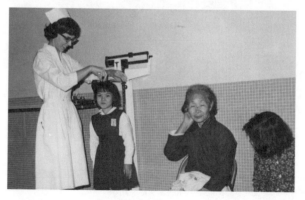

Dorothy checking height and weight of a young student.

Dorothy's first English Bible Class – 1963-1964. The girl on the far right
is Holly Wong.

Two nurses came to Hong Kong to work in the clinic. When the clinic
closed the two OMS nurses found other ministries. Marilyn Snider had a
burden to minister to children.   Dorothy went to Haven of Hope
Tuberculosis Hospital.

CHAPTER 15

KAU YAN MEDICAL CENTER

In November 1964 Harry Burr, director of Men For Missions International, and his wife, Eleanor, were in Hong Kong to celebrate laying the foundation stone for Kau Yan Medical Center. This was the second building in the project for which Men For Missions had raised money. What a joy to watch a dream come alive.

Kau Yan (Saving Grace) Medical Center was almost finished when Dr. Charles Omdal, his wife, Johanna, and their four children arrived in Hong Kong in May 1965.

It was a time of anticipation as the clinic building took shape and equipment purchased by Dr. Omdal and brought to Hong Kong was put in place. Following an application to the United States Relief Fund for aid in equipping our medical center, OMS was granted $35,000. On October 24, 1965, Kau Yan Medical Center was dedicated and two days later, right next door to the clinic, the foundation stone was laid for our largest church facility, Yan Poon (Grace Rock) Church. The ministry was growing and so were the facilities we had. It was a happy day when Phyllis Erny and I were able to begin putting some of our nursing skills to work.

We knew that to be more effective in our witness of Jesus' love and salvation to the patients who came to the clinic, we needed Christian Chinese nurses to work with us.

Betty was our first nurse. She had trained and worked in the Government Hospital in Hong Kong. She was not used to comforting patients and seeing them as people with emotional needs. Patients were numbers. When she saw how Dr. Omdal and the missionary nurses treated the patients, she was amazed. Betty was a Christian, but during her time with us she grew in grace and in the knowledge of Jesus. May and Joanna came a little later and were Dr. Omdal's right arm and translators. These nurses were wonderful with the children and ministered to many people. Our nurses went to several elderly patients living across the street in the H-block resettlement building to take their blood pressure and check on them.

I remember one seven-year-old boy Dr. Omdal found with the beginnings of pulmonary tuberculosis. He lived in another section of Kowloon, and his mother brought him to the clinic every day for his injection of streptomycin. After some time this little fellow began coming by himself on the bus to the clinic. In a very dignified manner, he would walk in, crawl up on the examining table, and wait until one of the Chinese nurses gave him his shot. He got well and his family came to the church for a while. We wished that everyone who came in the doors of the clinic would welcome Jesus into their hearts and lives. Unfortunately, such was not the case.

MARILYN SNIDER

1966-2000

In anticipation of the Kau Yan Medical Clinic growing, another nurse arrived in Hong Kong in December 1966. Marilyn Snider came from Muncie, Indiana, where she received her nurse's training at Ball State University. Her first major assignment was language study. Career missionaries in the Orient usually spent two long, grueling years studying the language. Even then, one had only touched the surface. After Marilyn's formal language study, she would be working in the clinic.

CLINIC MINISTRY

With the Men For Missions Crusade team, a special meeting held in the clinic waiting room included preaching, singing, and a time for the children. Invitations were sent to former patients and fifty chairs were set up for adults in one room and 100 chairs for children in another. But some 200 adults showed up and 500 children. People filled almost every corner of the clinic as they listened to the sharing of God's Word. That night six adults responded to the invitation to receive Jesus as their Savior.

In the years that the clinic was open, not only were many people helped physically, but also some found Jesus as their Savior and were baptized. We cannot put dollar amounts on the value of a soul. If in heaven the angels rejoice over one person who comes to Jesus (Luke 15:7), who are we to classify success or no success when things change?

When our doctor left, the time came to close the clinic. Because by that time the government had greatly increased their medical services, we were advised to phase out this part of our ministry. Since costs had increased more than anticipated, it seemed wise to heed our advisors. What would be done with the clinic building? For some time it housed a number of missionaries in slightly altered rooms. The single ladies had their living room in what was to have been the delivery room. Our green tile walls from floor to ceiling were cold and hard to decorate. The labor rooms became our bedrooms. I don't think we labored too much there. The sterilizing room was made into our kitchen. Later the third floor of the building that would have housed medical staff became the apartment for one of the families. This was good use of the space because the mission saved in rent money while we were seeking God's plan for us.

Some people thought that we had a "white elephant" on our hands, but here are some words by Priscilla Harrington in an article from the March 1984, *OMS Outreach*:

> *How could it be? After all the money and effort poured into that clinic, surely God wouldn't let it be wasted. But there it stood like a specter between church and school. Furthermore, with Hong Kong's accelerated construction, government schools soon replaced private ones. At the precise time, however, secondary schools became the colony's most pressing educational need. Where upon OMS, together with the Free Methodists and Schools For Christ Foundation, founded a high school. So instead of a white elephant, OMS possessed strategic land and buildings that with remodeling and new construction enabled the United Christian College to become a reality. Men For Missions' original $100,000 investment in concrete and steel continues to bear spiritual dividends in the lives of children and young people who have come to Christ.*

CHAPTER 16

DOROTHY BACKER LOANED TO HAVEN OF HOPE TUBERCULOSIS HOSPITAL

With the closing of the Kau Yan Medical Center, I was loaned to the 300-bed Haven of Hope Tuberculosis Hospital in the New Territories. Sister Annie Skau of the Mission Covenant Church of Norway founded Haven of Hope in 1955, and a number of missions staffed the hospital on a cooperative basis. It was truly an international team. We had English and Chinese doctors as well as Norwegian, Irish, American, English, and Chinese nurses. The rest of the staff came from all parts of China.

My assignment at the hospital, originally for a year, stretched into ten, 1968-1978. Those very interesting years working with Sister Annie, a Norwegian missionary nurse, were like being with a Hudson Taylor or any of the pioneer missionaries. Sister Annie had worked in northern China for 14 years. After the Communists came to power, she was still there. Everyone who knew her loved her, even some of the young Communist soldiers that she had taken care of when they were injured. She became very ill and was asked to leave because the Communists didn't want her to die there. She returned to Norway in 1951. Those early missionaries, like the Apostle Paul, knew the meaning of throwing themselves completely upon the Lord and His care.

Sister Annie returned to Hong Kong in 1953 and began to work among the refugee Nationalist soldiers who had fled China into Hong Kong. Many of these soldiers were hardened men. To keep them off Hong Kong streets, they were taken to an isolated place called Rennie's Mill, in the New Territories. Because of the years of fighting, many were very ill with tuberculosis and other diseases. God placed such a burden on Annie's heart for those who were sick in body and soul, and eventually Haven of Hope was born.

In the early 1960s, Annie took a little Chinese baby girl, born at the hospital of a mother who didn't want her. Annie adopted Ling Ling and today Ling Ling is a nurse in Norway, married with three little girls of her own. I learned so much in those years and will never forget the spiritual lessons Annie taught me.

One evening after work, I was standing with Annie on the bank overlooking the bay below with the moon brightly shining. She pointed to the moonlight path on the water and said, "God's love is just like the moonlight on the water; wherever you stand it comes directly to you." Now wherever I see moonlight on the water, I know God's love is flowing to me!

Several of the years I was at Haven of Hope, I worked with Mary Wong in Nursing Administration. By that time Sister Annie had retired and gone back to Norway after having a heart attack. Mary took over as Director of Nurses having worked with Annie for many years as her assistant. She loved the Lord and was a wonderful friend to me. As Mary's helper, I had the daunting task of being in charge when she was gone. Many of the older staff did not speak any English and they spoke Northern Chinese dialects, not the Cantonese dialect mainly spoken in Hong Kong. Someone said that Nurse Esther, from Shanghai, and I looked like a duck and chicken talking to one another, both talking fast and neither understanding the other. Much of the time that was true, but we both pretended we understood. Can you picture that?

One day we were preparing for a special baptismal service at the hospital. I recorded some of my thoughts on that day:

"Lord, don't let it rain! You know we've planned a baptismal service outside today." A heavy cloud threatened the worst as I hurried through morning routines. My thoughts kept turning to the nine patients who'd responded to Christian love here at Haven of Hope and were to be baptized that afternoon.

Opening my Living Bible, *my eyes fell on Joel 2:25: "For the rains he sends are tokens of forgiveness." What could be more appropriate on a baptismal day? "Okay, Lord, I'll like the rain."*

Assured, I took my place in the Easter morning service. Six lovely lily plants adorned the altar as sparrows chattered in the beams above. A soft haze enveloped the view of bay and hills beyond the chapel. Nurses and patients joined the sparrows in singing "Alleluia" and "Christ the Lord is Risen Today," before the message by Sister Annie, former Director of Nursing of Haven of Hope. She had returned for her 42nd spiritual birthday.

Outside, however, another complication developed. Slowly, through a loose plug, all the water drained from the children's swimming pool—

our makeshift baptistry. We'd have to start all over again. By four o'clock, the rains had passed and water gradually filled the pool. Observers circled the pool, and Pastor Hui spoke to the nine who'd met the requirements of baptism. One had come to us as a drug addict. Unwanted by his family, he'd tried to commit suicide by leaping from a building. Now, his life changed through Christ, he looked forward to a united home upon his hospital discharge.

Another, Mr. Lee, lived alone in Hong Kong, his wife and children still in China. He'd found a friend in Jesus. A young lady, victim of meningitis and tuberculosis, had first heard about God's love during her six-month hospital stay. We truly experienced "tokens of God's forgiveness" as one by one the nine knelt in the shallow water. Each one represented the showers of blessings God gives to us through His Son. His plans are perfect as He transforms turmoil into tranquility in individual lives.[20]

I can still see this picture in my mind even though many years have passed.

In June 1973 I was asked by Haven of Hope to take a course in tuberculosis and thoracic nursing in London, England. Because I was working with student nurses and English-trained nurses, they thought it would be helpful if I worked in a British hospital for a while. I spent six months in the Brompton Hospital in London, which specialized in diseases of the chest and heart. It was a great experience and I learned many new things. It would have been nice to see more of England, but it was time to return to Hong Kong. That was just before Christmas 1973, and I worked with the hospital until 1978. After my furlough I was reassigned by OMS to be the school nurse in United Christian College.

The Haven of Hope TB Hospital when Dorothy was there. The individual wards were named for the fruit of the Spirit, Love, Joy, Peace, Kindness, Goodness, and more.

Annie Skau, from Norway, became a mentor to Dorothy. She was truly a godly woman and dear friend.

Christmas is a special time at HOH. One of our elderly patients gets into the act. The wards get decorated and some are planning for the Christmas program in the chapel. The nurse with Dorothy has on the old fashioned cap. Those are mosquito nets tied up over the bed.

Dorothy taught this class English medical terms. She is still in touch with some of her former students.

CHAPTER 17

BEGINNING OF THE CHILDREN'S WORK

In an interview Dr. Ed Erny had with Marilyn Snider in 1972, she shared some of her inmost thoughts and burdens. "Talk about a mission field," she said, "just look across the street." From the OMS office and clinic building, one looked at a row of bunker-like "H" blocks separated from our property by no more than the narrow and winding Tong Yam Street.

"Here in Hong Kong," Marilyn explained, "35 percent of the population are under the age of 14. Within a radius of a block or so of us are 40,000 people, most of them children. Though we are reaching some of them through our primary schools, thousands of others have never heard the Gospel."

Although Marilyn initially came to Hong Kong to serve in the clinic, children were never far from her thoughts. "I'd see them every day crowding around the steps of the clinic, and I'd wonder why so little was being done to reach them. The burden kept growing. Then when OMS phased out the clinic, I knew God was saying, 'Okay, Marilyn, this is the opportunity you've been waiting for.'"

On her furlough Marilyn took special training in child evangelism and religious education. When she returned to Hong Kong, she got busy planning a pilot project—a series of child evangelism classes for neighborhood children. "I just wanted to prove that child evangelism can work in Hong

Kong," she said. "I was convinced it could be effective and could lead to solid results."

For five days 60 children came to the classes, sang Gospel songs, and followed the adventures of Bible heroes dramatized on story cards. By the last session 25 of the youngsters had received Christ and been personally counseled and enrolled in a special children's Bible correspondence course. Marilyn knew that their efforts were only the proverbial "drop in the bucket," but how could they broaden their base?

Teacher training was one way to begin. God brought two wonderful Chinese co-workers to help Marilyn. They began conducting a teacher training class each week at our Grace Rock Church. The teachers studied for three months and learned the basic techniques of child evangelism. Marilyn's goal was to eventually have classes for training teachers in every one of our churches. A big job, but we serve a big God! They also worked with the pastors and held some children's rallies. Marilyn worked hard to set up a library of tools on child evangelism. Books, stories, flannelgraph lessons, and other kinds of materials were put into a file so the churches could have a resource place.

The first young woman to help Marilyn came by a circuitous route that only the Lord could have worked out. Holly Wong, daughter of one of our early pastors, Wong Yuk Nan, had gone to nurses' training in the late '60s. Then she felt God leading her to go to seminary for more Bible training. In 1972 she had an assignment from her seminary class to work with the church. She went to her own church, Grace Rock Church, and talked to Rev. Ho about working with them in the summer. They didn't have anything for her then. As she left the church office, she walked downstairs past the OMS offices. There she "accidentally" met Marilyn.

Marilyn hadn't seen Holly for some time. As they chatted, Marilyn asked Holly if she was interested in helping her manage all the children's materials that she had brought from the USA. Holly helped her and did some translation of the materials into Chinese. Holly was happy because she had found the way to finish her seminary assignment. She remembers that Marilyn also asked her if during the summer she could help with a vacation Bible school on the Wong Tai Sin rooftop. OMS had a church there as well as the Bamboo Gardens Primary School.

Holly was very busy during that time preparing workshops to train teachers to teach Bible. She hoped to encourage young people to be trained to help with the children. One of the ladies in the Wong Tai Sin Church was Belle Ng Wai Ling. She helped Marilyn and Holly with the daily vacation Bible school in her church where she remains active today. Holly worked with Marilyn during each of her summer vacations from seminary and after she graduated, she came to work in the Children's Ministries until just before her daughter Karen was born.[21]

Two other ladies came to help: Ruth Li from our Yan Din Church and Virginia Fung who came from Taiwan with her husband, Sam, to help with the Lay Training Institute that OMS was trying to start. These ladies helped to lift a heavy load because the children's ministry was growing. There was so much to teach people and train them to work in their own churches. There were constant requests for materials. Marilyn did some teaching in one of the local Bible seminaries on the ministry to children. Gradually the work was transferred to each of the local HKEC churches to take care of their children and manage their camps. Marilyn's heart for children never left her even though later she ministered in other ways.

When I returned from my furlough, I was asked to do more with the HKEC and be a liaison between the churches and OMS. It was also my joy to work more closely with the Yan Shek Church (Zion). Because I had previously been the school nurse at UCC, with Marilyn taking over during my furlough, the change needed to meet with her approval to continue as the school nurse for UCC. This Marilyn did and the young people loved her. The English-speaking students especially spent a lot of time in the Medical Room. Marilyn also taught English Bible to several classes, and at one time her total number of Bible students was around 80. Writing exams, correcting papers, making grades, and being a nurse is a lot of work, but Marilyn did it.

Rev. Sonny Chow in front of Yan Ping "Grace and Peace" Home Help Center. The church members and other believers are reaching into the villages and to the elderly disabled, washing their clothes, taking a meal a day, and other helps.

CHAPTER 18

MORE CRUSADE WORK

Billy Campbell came to Hong Kong in the fall of 1965 as the fourth ECC crusader. Billy came from the UK with a heart burning for evangelism. He gives more details of the ECC team when he was a part of it:

The ECC team I worked with was located in the fishing village of Tai Po, not far from the China border. After a very basic two months full-time study of the Cantonese language, an interpreter was assigned to work alongside me on the team. Besides the regular programs of literature distribution and evening Gospel campaigns, we also gave encouragement and support to the two new congregations previously established in the New Territories at Kam Tin and Sheung Shui. Within a year, another church was planted as a result of ECC evangelism and ministry in Tai Po.

In 1966 the ECC team and Billy Campbell had the unprecedented opportunity to enter the "Closed Area," a belt of land about two miles wide along the China border, between Hong Kong and China. Billy said,

We were given a four-week permit to take clothing and other supplies to needy families in the Closed Area, but our aim was also to take "the Gospel to every creature" . . . I clearly recall in the experiences of those weeks -- a farmer busy in his rice paddy took time to listen to the Good News. In the next field where his wife was working, she also listened and took literature. Young boys and girls sheltering from the rain in the village hall eagerly read the gospel story in a colorful, illustrated booklet in Chinese. Children returning from school gathered around an age-old banyan tree where we held an open-air meeting. They learned choruses and listened attentively to the simple message of God and His love and salvation in Jesus. Even the old grandmothers and grandfathers showed interest in hearing about the risen Christ, the Savior of the world. We visited every home in the sections we were permitted to enter. Thousands of gospel portions and salvation leaflets were distributed. We were saddened by the sight of the barbed wire fencing separating that community of Hong Kong Chinese from the 1.3 billion Chinese in communist China to the north.

For a month the team covered the area distributing hundreds of gospel tracts and holding open-air meetings. A door had opened for them in spite of many adversaries. Many experiences strengthened the tug on Billy's heart for Hong Kong. By the end of his term he relates, "The call of God to return rang clear, but I had a need. I desired a helpmate. My trust was in the Lord, believing that He would lead to a partner of His choice." God did and he met a young lady from Wales during a convention in Scotland. He and Jeanne were married in August 1969, and after the usual deputation and funding they returned to Hong Kong in February 1970 to work in evangelism and youth ministries. God used them in a mighty way during their ministry. Their little daughter, Kathleen, was born in Hong Kong. When Kathleen was a young lady, she returned to Hong Kong in 1990 for a short term teaching English in the churches and helping wherever she could. Kathleen even met her future American Navy husband in Hong Kong. This place has captured the hearts of the Campbell family.[22]

How wonderful it is when those who have ministered for a short term return with a heart to share and work where God has called them. Billy joined Buddy Gaines, busy in evangelism and youth ministries. Buddy was another former Crusader who went home to the United States and met his wife, Martie Ewan. After Buddy finished his seminary training, the Gaines family—including two little daughters, Jodie and Angela—returned to Hong Kong in April 1969. A little later Mark came along, and then to complete their family, Matthew was born.

After Billy finished his time in Hong Kong as a Crusader, another young man from the United Kingdom, Bob Hale, arrived to take his place during the last part of 1968. As Hong Kong was gradually changing, some of the original methods used by the ECC team were no longer feasible. Bob found himself needing to be creative in looking for new approaches to evangelism. He worked in Sheung Shui, New Territories, for a while with Ng Yue Tong, and then came back into the city and worked with some of the city churches to encourage and help with evangelism. The OMS team loved and appreciated Bob. He was the last overseas missionary crusader for the Hong Kong ECC. He returned to England for further schooling and worked as a welfare social worker. I had the joy of attending the wedding of Shirley and Bob in London in the fall of 1973.

EVANGELISM EXPLOSION INTRODUCED TO HKEC & HONG KONG CHURCHES

While Buddy and Martie Gaines were on furlough in 1973, Buddy trained in an Evangelism Explosion Clinic presented by Dr. James Kennedy in Coral Ridge, Florida. He was very excited about the way this tool of evangelism more quickly motivated people to witness for Jesus Christ. In 1974 he introduced EE to our OMS-related churches, HKEC, and other Hong Kong churches, but it was not until 1978 that the first EE Clinic in Hong Kong took place. Buddy began training Brenda and Joseph Tsang Man Tung, who were working in OMS' first Reading Center in the Homantin Housing Estate. About 25,000 people lived in this area and needed to hear the Gospel.

What is EE? This is a ministry to glorify God by equipping local churches worldwide to multiply through friendship, evangelism, discipleship, and healthy growth. Spiritual multiplication results as EE continues in local churches.

EVERY CREATURE CRUSADE WORK CONTINUES

The ECC work has taken on different forms through the years to meet the needs of a changing world.

OMS Every Creature Crusade work played a very significant role in establishing Christian churches in Hong Kong that have now matured and grown, evangelizing and planting daughter churches throughout the Territory. The seven churches in the HKEC Conference in the mid-1970s, most of which were being at least partially financed by OMS, have now increased to almost 20 churches. All are pastored by theologically trained local Chinese, and 18 are fully self-supporting.

Today Rev. Tony Kwan coordinates every Creature Crusade work in Hong Kong. Tony is director of Development and Missions in the HKEC Conference. Born in Hong Kong in the mid-1950s, he committed his life to Christ when he was a teenager studying in a Christian school. After graduating from high school he went to Bradford, England, and received a master's degree in science, then went to Canada and completed a Master of Divinity degree at the Ontario Theological Seminary in Toronto.

In recent years in Hong Kong, ECC work has developed steadily. An ECC team planted the Yan Lam Church in Sheung Shui close to the China border in 1990. This church also serves as a family center with a very effective outreach work to the entire community. The church became fully indigenous in 1995. Yan Ping was their daughter church. Because of the heavy load on the believers in Yan Lam Church, the people in the small fellowship of Yan Ping were combined in the Yan Lam Church. The distance between the two locations is very short. The social ministry to the elderly and disabled continues from the Yan Ping Social Center.[23]

The Yan Ping Center is a unique ministry. The first time I visited this center, I wondered why there were two large washing machines, two dryers, and a large commercial kitchen. The helpers use bicycles instead of cars. This place of old villages where older people still live is in the northern part of the New Territories close to the border with China. The old and disabled have often been put on a shelf in Hong Kong contrary to popular opinion that the children always care for the elderly Chinese. With a very fast-paced population in Hong Kong and small living spaces, couples do not have a place to care for elderly family members and often they just do not care. What Rev. Sunny Chow had in mind when they applied for this center was to minister to these people nearby and in the villages.

The name Yan Ping means "grace and peace" and the grace and peace from our Lord is shared with these folks. The big kitchen prepares meals, and the large washers and dryers wash clothes for those who cannot do it anymore. The van that the Lord provided through His people takes the bicycles, food boxes, and helpers to the villages. Cars cannot get into the small pathways, making bicycles the best means of transportation. The elderly and disabled are so grateful for the caring and practical help, and certainly this is what God wants done. The church didn't take hold because of the type of people in the immediate area. The people from Yan Lam Church, a thriving congregation, continue with the ministry at Yan Ping, which is within walking distance.

Yan Ho Church in the Homantin Resettlement Housing district of Kowloon was started at the end of 1991 and is now also fully indigenous. During the week the facilities are used as a Reading Center giving contact with many students and opportunities to evangelize among them. Yan Ho Church and two other recent church-plants, the Yan Tin and Yan Yat Churches, were started using the mother-daughter church-plant model, but also with helpful ECC team involvement.

Yan Tin is a daughter church of Grace Church, Yan Poon an outgrowth of the very first chapel begun in 1954, and Yan Yat a daughter church of Yan Ying.

All this represents exciting growth and development of the church in Hong Kong at the beginning of the 21st century. The pioneering/church-planting Every Creature Crusade ministry of the 1950s and '60s has produced indigenous congregations—self-governing, self-supporting and self-propagating. Most churches have purchased their facilities (apartments on first and second floors in a high-rise building) and support their own pastors.[24]

THE VISION FOR ECC IN HONG KONG IN THE 21ST CENTURY

The vision for ECC work in Hong Kong is to evangelize at every opportunity. Of Hong Kong's 6.5 million people, 25 percent are under the age of 25. A young man from one of the HKEC churches has taken over the leadership of a "Teen Mission" outreach to troubled Chinese youth in an expanding satellite city in the New Territories. Discussions are taking place about the possibility of appointing an ECC team to work in evangelism in a "special needs" area of ministry.

The flow of new arrivals from China into Hong Kong is a challenge to the Christian church to reach out to these unreached people. Chinese citizens have been many years under the godless atheism of Communism, so their thinking is totally different from the Hong Kong Chinese who have lived in a free zone. This presents a wonderful opportunity to share the Gospel with those who have never heard the name of Jesus.[25]

Another exciting ministry taking place is OMS-HKEC involvement with the Filipino population in Hong Kong. Thousands of young women and a smaller number of young men have come from the Philippines to work as domestic helpers. Many are educated and married with children, but all this has been left in the Philippines while one member of the family comes to Hong Kong to earn some money. With the poor economy in the Philippines, those leaving home to work as domestics around the world bring money back into that land. These Filipinos have no place where they belong and so they seek out one another. Several mission groups have begun a ministry with the domestic workers and the response is great. Now OMS is involved. The new ECC budget for HK has been approved and in the fall of 1999, a worker came from the Philippines and the OMS Faith Fellowship in Manila to start a Filipino Fellowship in Hong Kong. God's ways lead in directions that those who began the work would never have imagined.

Rev. Tony Kwan, Director of ECC work in Hong Kong with Dr. David Long, OMS HK missionary.

CHAPTER 19

YOUTH MINISTRIES

In the '70s and early '80s, under Field Director Grant Nealis' able leadership, a creative method of reaching more youth and establishing more churches came into being. OMS and the HKEC applied to the Hong Kong government for one of the new reading center spaces in a new housing estate being built. These empty bays on the ground floor were closed in and set up with the needed furnishings for young people to come and study. We obtained three reading/study centers and a center for the elderly to come during the day. Churches came from each of these government resources.

Grant reported in 1972 on the increasingly important outreach to the youth of Hong Kong, the group most responsive to the Good News:

Since the Every Creature Crusade program had run its effective course, we more and more geared our evangelistic outreach to young people. The program we began with funds from Total Advance Now (TAN) was a camp for our sixth grade graduates and a camp that the conference Youth Commission planned for the HKEC young people. Our primary schools gave us a natural evangelistic outreach. Each school had an entire Christian faculty and the principal was a graduate of our OMS Bible Seminary. Every week the children had

127

two periods of programmed Bible instruction and two chapel services. During those years special evangelistic services were often conducted. After the sixth-graders completed their government examinations for entrance to middle school and before their own school's final exams, the OMS with TAN funds sponsored a camp for these sixth-graders as a final effort to harvest the fruit from the seed that had been sown for six years.

As supervisor of the schools, Grant found those sixth-grade graduate camps invaluable. They helped reap the fruit for which people had prayed and worked a long time. The camp was considered the crowning climax of their primary school learning experiences.

Beginning in 1970 the OMS sponsored its first evangelistic youth camp. Each Christian brought a non-Christian friend. The first year we had contact with about 75 non-Christians of which 34 accepted Christ.

A highlight each year for fifth-grade students at the OMS school was a week at the huge YMCA campsite overlooking an inlet of the South China Sea. A major problem that confronted the missionary counselors at that time was the shortage of Bibles for the campers. This was a matter for prayer. Just before the next camp, Eric Wong, a Hong Kong businessman and a Gideon, brought 400 New Testaments with Psalms for the fifth and sixth-grade OMS students. Gideon International Executive Director M.A. Henderson was in Hong Kong for the presentation. This was in the summer of 1972. At the close of one of the evening assemblies, over half the young people stood, indicating their desire to know more about Jesus.[26]

Billy and Jeanne Campbell were involved in Evangelism and Youth Ministries and Jeanne tells of all the "challenges" that came their way during the intense planning for an evangelistic barbecue. The problems ranged from the endless phone calls, "wrong numbers," to an encounter with the police, an empty gas tank on one of their scooters, and no key to the gas tank. For two months they had been planning this time with their English Bible class at the Tai Well Po Church. The Lord brought peace out of chaos and the young people brought friends. After lots of eating, laughter, and fun, the message of salvation in Christ was given and these young people heard about Jesus. There would be more good days like these.[27]

From 1972-1974 the emphasis moved from OMS sponsoring the camps to each of the Hong Kong Evangelical Churches having its own camp.

While Buddy and Martie Gaines were home on furlough, Buddy was rallying prayer and financial support to plan a full-fledged Youth Ministries Department under OMS and the HKEC.

In an August 1974 prayer letter, Grant said:

David Tsang who finished his study at Asbury Seminary and the Buddy Gaines family are returning to Hong Kong this month. Buddy and David will be making an all-out effort to reach the young people through youth rallies, spiritual life retreats, a coffee house ministry, and discipling believers in lay training classes. Our ministry to high school youth is promising. United Christian College already has a full registration for the Form

I classes (seventh grade) that we are opening on September 6, 1974.

Because of the enthusiastic spiritual response among youth, we sensed God's leading to convert our medical building and primary school into a high school. After two years of deliberating, the government approved in principle a 1,000-student school and agreed to underwrite 84 percent of the capital costs. The Free Methodist Church and a body of Chinese Christians called "Schools For Christ Foundation" assisted us in the operation of the school.[28]

The rooftop schools were gradually phased out because the government found a new source of revenue and started collecting rent for the use of the rooftops. Chung Yan Primary School began moving the younger students to other schools in preparation for the opening of the new high school. The fifth and sixth-graders moved into the first classes of the new United Christian College, which was to be junior high and high school.

In 1975 OMS Hong Kong purchased a flat in the Rose Court apartments on Rose Street in Yau Yat Chuen, Kowloon. This was a first for OMS to own housing in Hong Kong. From 1984-1987, Dale and Polly McClain came back to Hong Kong to fill in as field director for a term. The Nealis family returned to the United States at that time. More housing was purchased on Beacon Hill, Alnwyck Road, in an apartment complex called "Joy Garden."

130

CHAPTER 20

UNITED CHRISTIAN COLLEGE

United Christian College (UCC) was formally registered with the government as a non-profit Chinese high school in 1974. It opened in September with seven Form One (seventh-grade) classes and 11 staff members. Dr. Paul Hau-lim Pang, director of Schools for Christ, was the first principal and Grant Nealis, the school's first supervisor.

By 1976, 862 students were enrolled in 19 classes. Because of a shortage of classrooms, the school temporarily changed to two sessions daily. With an approved capital grant from the Hong Kong Government, construction began on two new buildings in the spring of 1976.

They demolished the old clinic building first. It was more cost-effective to get rid of the old building and start new than to try to remodel the existing one. A new five-story block held the special classrooms such as music, geography, art, chemistry, and biology. The other building was comprised of ordinary classrooms built at the base of the hill. This made the OMS property look like a huge square from above. The remodeled Chung Yan Primary School was on the west side and the new special classrooms block on the north side. Grace Rock Church closed the east side, and the new classrooms building formed the south side close to the mountain. The playground was in the open center where a basketball court was marked out. Two covered playground areas were under two of the blocks.[29]

The new buildings for United Christian College were completed by September 1977 and dedicated for the Lord's use in October. These buildings gave us more classroom space, which was soon being used to capacity.

This time of construction was a most difficult time for teachers and students. There were no air-conditioned classrooms in those early days. (Dave Aufrance recalls that the noise and pounding of the pile drivers right next to his classroom was so horrendous that he was ready to leave Hong Kong.)

REV. & MRS. MELVIN KIZER
1974-1983

Rev. and Mrs. Melvin Kizer came from Indiana to Hong Kong in December 1974 to supervise the building construction. Besides their work in the construction, Nancy helped with secretarial tasks in the OMS office. Mel and Nancy were assigned to the Ko Chiu Road Reading Center and they helped with the new Yan Ying Church that began with the people who attended the Reading Center.

Because of their love for the young people, Mel led a weekly Bible study for the young men and Nancy had a class for teenage girls, teaching them English, cooking, and Bible with the goal to reach them for Christ. They loved entertaining them in their home. After the Kizers resigned from OMS in 1983 and returned to the States, Nancy was diagnosed with cancer. She loved the Lord and serving Him was her joy. She is enjoying His presence now.[30]

DAVID & CYNTHIA AUFRANCE
1975-2000

About this time a new young couple arrived in Hong Kong to teach at United Christian College (UCC) and to work with the youth. David and Cynthia Aufrance arrived in September 1975. They came to us from the Evangelical Friends Church – Eastern Region.

Dave grew up near Alliance, Ohio, and Cindy was raised in Amish country, Berlin and Walnut Creek, Ohio. They met at Malone College where Dave majored in Music Education and Cindy majored in Psychology.

Dave's first assignment after arriving in Hong Kong was teaching Oral English, Music, and Bible at UCC, where he taught until 1990.

Dave and Cindy came to UCC at the beginning of the school's second year as a junior high and high school. They only had Forms One and Two (Grades 7 & 8) and met in the former Chung Yan Primary School building. Cindy taught for two years at UCC and then worked in the OMS office for a while as secretary for Buddy Gaines, acting field director, until Dave and Cindy's daughter, Rebecca, was born in March 1978.

The Aufrances lived in the old Kau Yan clinic building for the first months that they were in Hong Kong. Dave remembers that first Christmas time as very cold. The rooms in the clinic where they were living were so big, the only way they could get warm after they came home from school was to go to bed and try to warm up under the covers. Remember, the living room was formerly the tiled delivery room and the bedrooms had been the labor rooms.

Smoking, stinking kerosene heaters were the other alternative and they warmed only one spot at a time.

In January 1976 they moved to Yau Yat Chuen to OMS' first residential property on Rose Street, a large third-floor flat that had a fourth-floor apartment attached. A former owner had built the fourth-floor apartment on top of the original building.

On the third floor the large apartment was remodeled into two smaller, completely contained apartments for the single ladies. Mary Ellen Beetley and Marilyn Snider were the first occupants on third floor, and the Aufrances occupied the fourth floor. This property was only about ten minutes walk from the OMS offices, Grace Church, and UCC. It was a 15-minute ride to the old airport, compared to ride of 45 minutes to an hour to the new airport.

To find housing in this area was one of God's many provisions for OMS-HK as the property was usually very expensive and in a high-class residential area. Maybe one of the drawbacks was that the final approach to the Kai Tak Airport runway was right over the top of the building. The big planes were so low that one could count the rivets and read the writing on the underside. Needless to say, it was a noisy blast when a plane went over.

MORE OF UNITED CHRISTIAN COLLEGE—
UCC MEDICAL ROOM

In 1979 one of the ground-level, smaller storage rooms was converted into a medical room. This facility and service relieved the teachers of the burden of teaching a class and caring for a sick student at the same time. What do Band-Aids, thermometers, and health-room facilities have to do with winning the kids of UCC for Jesus? Here's a report about one of my days in the medical room:

It started when a teacher brought Wing Ting to my office. He had a fight with a classmate in his schoolroom. Cleaning up scratches on his face gave me time to talk and try to calm him. Wing Ting was 12 years old and had been under a psychiatrist's care for about two years. He had been able to cope fairly well with classes, but his behavior was strange and his classmates didn't like him. Wanting to go home, he phoned his mother. Whatever she said to him angered him so much that he threw down the telephone and would have rushed outside had I not stopped him at the door.

About that time Chi Ming returned to the medical room because his head hurt. Earlier he had fallen and hit his head on the asphalt playground, playing ball in physical education class. Suddenly he became nauseated and sick. Oh my, was this a serious head injury? The interruption shifted Wing Ting's attention. He calmed down and helped me with Chi Ming. Wing Ting's mother came to take him home, and at the same moment the ambulance I had called for arrived.

Wing Ting did not come back to school as the doctor said he was unable to cope. He heard about Jesus here at UCC, that Jesus loves and cares for him. I prayed that the name of Jesus would penetrate his confused mind and that Wing Ting would let Jesus help him. I will never know, but Jesus does.

*As I waited with Chi Ming in the hospital until
family came, I had time to talk to him about our
Savior. "Since you have been at UCC have you ever
asked Jesus to come into your heart?"*

"Sort of."

*So I took advantage of the time to water the seed
that had already been sown in this boy's heart.*

*God promises harvest if we are faithful in our
sowing and watering. Band-Aids seemed to be a
good evangelistic tool for me.*[31]

In 1979 the Hong Kong Government offered subsidy
to many schools, including UCC. A school accepting the
subsidy would forfeit the internal power to hire and fire
according to its own principles as well as other restrictions.
In order to retain the founding principles, the school
decided not to accept the subsidy from the government.
Many outsiders thought that we would be sorry and would
not be able to give our teachers a good salary. The teachers,
who all loved the Lord, were willing to stand by the
decision of the UCC Board of Directors and let God work
out His details. As a matter of fact, God did far more than
we could ever have asked or thought. Eventually our
teachers were paid the same level as other schools and God
gave many other joys to the school, students, and staff
because we stayed true to God's ways.

The 1980s brought many changes and a lot of
progress to UCC. The student body average was about
1,200 and eventually upper level classes were added, Forms
6 and 7. The American equivalent would be grades 12 and
13 or junior college level. All students had to sit for the

136

Hong Kong School Leaving Certificate exams after Form 5 (Grade 11). If they received good marks on those exams they were eligible for the upper level classes. Good reports also assured the students a greater opportunity to enter one of Hong Kong's universities.

A new English stream was added to UCC in 1981. The new students who were accepted into the new Form One class (Grade 7), had to be able to function in English. David Aufrance was the homeroom teacher for these students and followed them the first three years. Dave recalls that those young people came from many different countries with families from all walks of life. We could remember students from 12 countries: Korea, Japan, Philippines, India, Brunei, Malaysia, Thailand, New Zealand, Sri Lanka, Seychelles, United States, and Canada. These kids brought with them a multitude of different beliefs. But to attend UCC, they were required to take the Bible class and attend chapel. We called them the ACE students because they used the Accelerated Christian Education curriculum for their English classes. All their other subjects were taken with the Chinese students in regular classes. In the school each level or grade had several classes. Form One (Grade 7) had six classes—A to F. The E class was the English stream and, of course, taught in English. Depending on whether the teacher came from Britain or America, determined which English the kids learned. They all proved to be very versatile. The Chinese students who had a higher comprehension of English were also part of the E class. We literally had a mission field within our doors.

Dr. Pang left UCC to become president of the Research Institute for Christian Education in 1985 and Dr.

David Chi Shang To succeeded him as principal. As the school expanded more space was needed.

In 1987 we had groundbreaking for another new building to be built on a postage stamp-size plot located just behind the church building next to the rocky hill. Mel Kizer returned to Hong Kong once again to supervise the building. This was a joint project with OMS International and Schools for Christ Foundation. Dr. Pang had envisioned a tall building there that would house OMS offices, Research Institute offices, some classrooms for UCC, and other possibilities. Any available land in Hong Kong was precious. The new ten-story Christian Education Center was dedicated in April 1989 and continues to be used to the maximum. OMS offices are on the ninth floor and the Training Center is on the eighth. In the year 2000, OMS opened the new seminary with several class modules being taught on the eighth floor.

DR. DAVID CHI SHANG TO— PRINCIPAL OF UCC

United Christian College made some significant changes before 1997. Some of them were very insightful. Following is part of an interview with Principal David To in early March 1999:

I came to the school in 1977, the third year after the school was started. I was appointed principal in 1985 upon my return from Canada and my studies there in Toronto. I did my doctoral studies from 1981-84. All along I worked with Dr. Paul Pang, the first principal and one of the co-founders of the school.

One of the interesting things that happened during my service at UCC was starting the English-speaking stream in 1981. Then in 1997, because of the change over from British sovereignty to China, the Chinese government instigated a Special Administrative Region (SAR) in Hong Kong. Our school then experienced a major change, psychologically, in terms of the school ethos, our characteristic and distinguishing attitudes, habits and beliefs. Before the changeover, we had to do something to make the kids aware of the changeover. The colonial system was going to end. British rule would be gone and we would be living under the Chinese government. Although it is an autonomous region, still the sovereignty belongs to China and we became part of the homeland. We really had to make the kids aware that they were studying in a Chinese school. They had to learn to sing the Chinese national anthem and learn more about China, the existing government, and maybe some ideology of Communism. We had to do something about civic education before the return, then after the return this kind of thing goes on.

All this was new to the teachers because they had to learn the meaning of the national flag, the regional flag, and how to place all those things.

In terms of the school atmosphere there was some change, but in terms of teaching curriculum there was only one change, those things related to the colonial system. Some names were changed and we had to use a different concept. In terms of the pure science subjects and in terms of language, there was no change.

The other thing that was a drastic difference and had a great impact on the school was the phasing out of the English program we started in 1981. The program was basically started to help the missionary children have a place to study in a Christian atmosphere. After several years the missionaries and the school discovered that this wasn't the best for their children because the school was not an American program but a local Hong Kong program. The modification only went as far as the language learning, using the English. When the missionary children returned to the States for studies, they found some problems. If they studied in the International schools in Hong Kong, there was no problem in the transfer.

The English program students declined from about 60 to about a dozen and we wondered if we should close the program. But about that time there was a large influx of returning overseas Chinese. They saw that our program was good for their children. Some could not pay the high tuition of the International schools and some wanted their children to learn more Chinese. They began to ask about our school. We had many applications from the Indian population, but it was about the same time that many Chinese were returning. We tended to accept the overseas Chinese because they could speak Chinese although not read it and they fit in faster. Instead of closing down we began to refocus our student body and target the returned overseas Chinese. We made some changes in our English program and began using English materials more suited to Hong Kong. These materials were being used in the International Christian School. The student numbers in the English program grew to about 110.

Then in 1998, related to the changeover, some people in the government were pushing for total teaching in the mother tongue, that is Cantonese Chinese. So they forced most of the schools to use Chinese as the teaching medium in the junior forms. We fought to keep the English program, going to the Education Department three times, but they refused us. So from September 1998-99, we phased out Form 1 (Grade 7) of the English program. In a few years the program will be completely phased out. To me this is a great pity because the Hong Kong Education Department was too rigid and could not see the benefit of this program. Well, some did see it but they couldn't do much about it. The policy was set.

The return of Hong Kong to China has not had a very great effect on the local schools. Schools with Christian backgrounds continue with what they have been doing. The government has not made any rules to limit religious freedom in the schools. The Bible curriculum can still be taught. The basic change is the mentality that now we teach the children that they are Chinese citizens living in their own land; they should love their country. People in Hong

141

Kong see country and the Communist Party as two separate entities. We will teach the kids to love the country but not to love the party. In China mainland, the Chinese government sees these two entities as the same thing, inseparable. With more Western leanings in Hong Kong we know that parties can be changed.

So far we have the freedom to make our curriculum and we can still spread the Gospel to the students. When the students graduate, the percentage of those who have become Christians while at UCC seems to remain around the 60 percent mark.

Since these words are from a Chinese man, one can gain a better perspective about some of the subtleties of the change over from British rule to China rule.

OMS Field Director Dave Aufrance wrote in August 1998:

In the spring I reported the fact that the Education Department was forcing most schools to go to the Chinese medium of instruction. United Christian College was one of those. It left only 20 percent of the elite schools with the right to use English as the medium of instruction. Polls indicated that between 70 and 90 percent of the parents (depending on which poll) wanted their children to be in schools that used English as the medium of instruction. The fact that the government forced the issue against the wishes of most of the people was one of the reasons its popularity lagged.

The government has continued to be isolated from the "real people" of Hong Kong and only listens to those advisors that tend to tickle their ears with the things they want to hear. Hong Kong is still a very special place, but it seems that some of the things that have made Hong Kong the great and free economic city it is are starting to fall by the wayside.

In April 1999 UCC celebrated its 25th anniversary with many activities. Rev. Gery Helsby, former OMS field director (1988-91) and chairman of the UCC Board, was able to return for this occasion and was the special speaker during the celebration ceremony. We are so thankful to God for His hand on the school through these years.

Since Hong Kong came under China sovereignty, some interesting events have taken place. UCC and Dr. To were introduced to a school in China near Qinghai Lake in Qinghai Province. This area is economically poor and some children cannot afford to go to school. UCC, through the Board of Directors and donations from teachers and students, helped to build a dormitory for the school. Now through the same avenue, teachers and students from UCC in Hong Kong are supporting a number of these children.

INTERNATIONAL CHRISTIAN SCHOOL (ICS)

During Gery Helsby's time as OMS field director, 1988-1991, he and a missionary from another mission began thinking about beginning a school for missionary children. They formed a board to look into all the ramifications of such a venture, and everything seemed to

143

come together at the right time and place. There are six sponsoring missions: OMS International, SEND International, China Free Methodist Mission, Eastern Mennonite Mission, the Southern Baptists, and the Conservative Baptists. In 1991 Gery was asked to go to OMS Headquarters in Greenwood, Indiana, to take the position of vice president of Homeland Ministries under Dr. J. B. Crouse. When Gery left Hong Kong, a big burden fell on Dave Aufrance, who was also in the beginning stages of planning.

In 1992 the school opened with grades 7-11 and about 56 students. They began with a US$200,000 loan from Morrison Academy, a school for missionary children in Taiwan. The first year the school broke even, and within two years the loan was paid back. In 1993 the school's second year, grade 12 was added as well as an elementary school. Enrollment has continued to increase over the years. In 1997 a second elementary school was added. ICS enrollment is now more than 400 students, with a waiting list of nearly that many. The school is looking to expand to accommodate the many students who would like to attend.

Applications and proposals have been made to the Hong Kong Education Department several times for loans and land grants, but none has been granted at the time of this writing. Dave Aufrance is chairman of the Board of Directors as well as OMS field director. The majority of the teachers, all Christians and native English speakers, come from the USA and Canada.

Twenty-one countries are represented at the school. About ten percent of the students come from the western missionary community and about 20 percent from full-time returning Chinese Christian workers. The rest of the students come from the business and university population in Hong Kong. Regardless of religious background, all students are required to take Bible class. As students hear the Good News and see the love of Christ in the faculty and staff, many make decisions to follow Christ. The teachers then follow through with nurturing and helping the students to mature in their faith.

Rev. Ho and his son, pastor of one of the ECC churches.

The daughter church of Yan Din "Double Grace" Church in Fanling, Wah Ming Housing Estate.

UNITED CHIRSTIAN COLLEGE
The Chinese writing on the left means:
Jesus is the Way, the Truth, and the Life.

The students in their PE uniforms making the letters of UCC.

CHAPTER 21

CREATIVE WAYS TO BEGIN CHURCHES— READING CENTERS

A youth outreach began in the new housing development called Homantin. About 25,000 people were moved into this high-rise concentration. The government leased OMS 1,300 square feet on the ground floor to operate an air-conditioned reading-study room for the secondary students from these hot, crowded homes. Joseph and Brenda Tsang, recently married and with seminary training behind them, were assigned to do personal work among those who came. Joseph was a product of our Second Church, Yan Yue, and Mary Ellen Beetley had taught him in her English Sunday school class.

Since purchasing land on which to build a church was not an option, we sought God in prayer for other ways. God opened the way for OMS to apply for a reading center. What are these centers and where are they? As the housing needs grew in Hong Kong and new housing estates were built, the Government Social Welfare Department planned in advance which social services were needed in that area. Near the OMS offices and school a new housing estate replaced the old "H" blocks built in the early '50s. The service planned for that estate was a large kindergarten. The financial and personnel resources for such a large undertaking was not possible for OMS, but the mission's application was granted for a reading center in the Homantin Estate.

When OMS began, what the center would look like was still a dream. All we saw were two open bays underneath about 20 stories of apartments. We had to close in those bays and put in everything needed for a comfortable reading and study room. We also were required to meet government regulations. In trying to plan for new churches in certain areas, OMS applied for several centers in different locations. These applications were not always granted, which meant we were somewhat at the mercy of the Government Social Welfare Department in opening new areas.

Why the need for a reading study center? Didn't the people have new apartments? Yes, but 400-600 square feet of apartment housed six to eight family members. Often neighbors were noisy, playing loud music or mahjong incessantly, making space for concentrated study difficult to find at home. The center was a quiet and cool place of escape, an air conditioner relieving the awful humid heat. It was a friendly place with someone who would care and listen. In the first year that we opened two reading centers, one in Homantin and one on Ko Chiu Road near Yau Tong Estate, more than 400 students found refuge and peace for concentrated study by registering at OMS centers for a token fee.

The centers offered another kind of peace as well—peace with God. The reading center attendant, whether Chinese, Western missionary, or pastor, became a friend to the students. Counseling, camping programs, rallies, English conversation opportunities, and an introduction to

Jesus Christ awaited each young person who indicated interest. Goals for the reading centers included evangelization of the families of students and the establishment of a church in that area.

THE SOCIAL CENTER FOR THE ELDERLY

OMS was not able to get any more reading/study centers for some years. But God opened up another kind of center and another kind of ministry. Psalm 71:9 says, "Do not cast me away when I am old; do not forsake me when my strength is gone."

This has been the plight of many elderly people in Hong Kong. Families are busy and flats are small, so caring for an elderly relative is a hardship for many. When this center became available, OMS felt God's leading in a new direction to begin a new church.

On November 7, 1982, 200 mostly elderly folks, crowded into two small rooms to witness the opening of the OMS International Social Center for the Elderly. This was in the Tai Hing Estate in Tuen Mun, New Territories. The young pastor welcomed his guests, old people who proudly displayed membership cards to show they belonged. Many of these folks came from an elderly hostel located in another high-rise nearby.

This center was situated on the ground floor of a huge 30-story high-rise building, prime space that according to the government must have a social service. "Our ultimate goal is always to reach people for Christ," Grant Nealis explained. "But we start where there is a need." Opening a new church in Hong Kong is usually tied to opening a new work.[32]

The Center for the Elderly was certainly a new work for OMS. Up to that time most of our efforts were directed toward ministry with young people. Doing this kind of social work was not in our plans. But it must have been part of God's plan because we watched Him pull circumstances and people together at just the right time. *"For my thoughts are not your thoughts, neither are your ways my ways," declares the Lord. "As the heavens are higher than the earth, so are my ways higher than your ways and my thoughts than your thoughts"* (Isaiah 55:8,9).

Funding a large venture is difficult but our Hong Kong Evangelical Church Conference (HKEC) wanted to have a part. They volunteered to purchase the equipment and furnishings required. They reached their goal in six months. How great to have this confirmation of God's leading. Now we needed to find God's man for this new work. Another praise … he found us!

REV. SONNY CHOW KA SHING

Chow Ka Shing (Sonny) had been pastoring for a couple of years after graduating from seminary. He felt a restlessness in himself "to go to the neediest place and serve." He learned that we needed someone for a pioneer work and knew that OMS stressed evangelism, high on his list of priorities.

In November 1999 the center had its 17th anniversary. The elderly do not live there, but come as they like during the day and evening hours. They have a membership so that the center can control the numbers coming and going. They have birthday parties, outings via buses, worship services, counseling, etc. They learn new things like Chinese shadow boxing, cooking, and chess. They can just sit and watch television or chat with friends.

Does this really fill a need? One old gentleman told us he had been evicted from his tin-wood-cardboard hut. Age and poor health prevented him from joining his family in Singapore. Some Christian friends helped him secure a bunk in a home for the aged. He is grateful for a place to sleep but dislikes the constant press of noise and people. That's why he likes to come to the center. "It's so peaceful and quiet here," he said. "The best part is that someone cares enough to give us a place of our own."

It takes time to build a church. Many of the elderly are clinging to the old customs and beliefs. It is hard, but not impossible to change the habits of a lifetime.

When one of the elderly believers gives testimony to their faith in baptism, there is much clapping and joy. For the last few years their church average has been around 55. It has been difficult to grow the church with the elderly and youth members and to get into the lives of the working people who live in that area. Many still cling to the old beliefs just as much as their elders. With the pastor, Christian social worker, and staff the light continues to shine there in that housing estate of Tai Hing, Tuen Mun. The church is called Yan Fook, (Blessings of Grace).

Rev. Sonny Chow has been a very hard worker. After the Center for the Elderly was well established, he asked if there was another pioneer opportunity for him within the HKEC. We had applied to the government for another center and were given a Family Service Center in Sheung Shui, a growing town very near the Hong Kong-China border. OMS had a small chapel there in the late '60s, but was closed for lack of growth. Now a brand new opportunity and pioneer work presented itself to us. As far as we know this Family Center was the first of its kind in Hong Kong. We had to have social workers, counselors, people to work with mothers, and people to work with children and the whole family. Hong Kong people did not share their needs or problems before, but just as the world has changed, so have the people in Hong Kong. Some began to come for marriage counseling. Women came who had been abused, fathers came, and families brought their children for before and after-school care. Rev. Chow and his Christian staff were in charge of all this. The work at the Family Service Center really grew and out of it came a new church they called Yan Lam (Grace Raining Down).

In the fall of 1989, Rev. Chow, chairman of the HKEC Conference, and several other pastors and OMS field directors went to Seoul, Korea, on a study tour. The revival and growth of the Korean OMS churches greatly challenged our people. They came back full of excitement and determination to advance for God.

During the time in Korea, Rev. Chow began having nosebleeds for no apparent reason. On return to Hong Kong he had a medical check-up. After several tests, the diagnosis was cancer of the nose and throat. When he got the report he was very shocked and afraid, but in his own words, he said, "At that very moment the comforting voice of the Holy Spirit whispered His peace." Sonny added:

I took courage as I recalled the sufferings of Job, the thorn of Paul, the three journeys of Valetta Steel Crumley through the valley of darkness (Thrice Through The Valley is her story of God's grace through the loss of her whole family. This book is available through the OMS office), *and the challenge to death of Josephine Yan-Yui So.* (The founder of Breakthrough, a well-known Christian organization in Hong Kong, she suffered with cancer for 20 years.) *They led me onto the path of faith. God proved His grace and power sufficient and perfect in my weakness. Through the prayers and care of brothers and sisters of OMS churches, God provided treatment at a hospital known for its effective cancer treatment. And during the 30 sessions of radiotherapy He reduced my physical suffering to a minimum. "Even though I walked through the valley of the shadow of death I feared no evil."*

God's grace has been extended to me in many ways, and I wanted to bear witness of the response to many prayers on my behalf. Also of great significance are the spiritual lessons God gave me through the illness. I want to share four truths:

***Suffering** is commonplace in life and must be faced by man whether he be noble or humble. The Bible says, "Yet man is born to trouble as surely as sparks fly upward" (Job 5:7). Even Jesus had to suffer when He was on earth. But God has promised us peace in such experiences.*

***Suffering** is not limited to sickness. Political oppression, economic recession, death and spiritual struggle are also sufferings. Whichever form it takes, suffering can lead into deeper spiritual life in which we experience the close intimacy of God and reliance on His grace.*

Suffering multiplies our witness and usefulness. Through it God comforts and teaches us His purposes. The Bible says: "(God) comforts us in all our troubles, so that we can comfort those in any trouble with the comfort we ourselves have received from God" (1 Corinthians1:4).

Suffering contains not only the negative sense of curse and punishment but also has a positive meaning and value. It cultivates a thankful heart, which allows God to complete good deeds through suffering. At the same time, we learn to turn our wounds into strengths, and let others know of God's love and transforming power.

To God's glory and in response to many of your prayers, I have now been given a clean bill of health from my doctor and have had no further problem.[33]

It was a blessing that Sonny didn't experience any more problems with the cancer. That wasn't the story of another dear brother and pastor of Yan Shek Church, Rev. Simon Lee. When I returned from furlough in the fall of 1989, my assignment changed from being school nurse to having more contact with our HKEC churches. I was to act as liaison between OMS and the churches. Also I began to help at Yan Shek Church (Zion). Pastor Lee and his wife, Miu, were very young. Simon was 21 years old when he began with youth work at Yan Shek, and in 1988 at the age of 24 he was voted in as the senior pastor. God had given Simon a burden and love for the people and as he had studied in seminary, he was diligent to learn. His preaching was deep, biblical, and drew people to Jesus. I loved to hear him and understood most of his words as he preached.

While at Zion, I played the piano for the little choir and had a fellowship with the young single women and a small Bible study in English with a couple of housewives. The pastor's wife, Miu, came along to be a helper. A number of times I was in the Lees' home for a meal, and the fellowship was sweet and precious to me for they became very dear. Even though there were many years of age and culture between us, God united our hearts in a special relationship.

Simon died of cancer that had spread all through his body in September 1997. I returned to Hong Kong for a visit in November and surely missed seeing Simon but was able to spend a little time with Miu and her two little boys.

Because many people ask the same questions when someone dies an untimely death, at least to our way of seeing, I am going to share some of the words that came from the Hong Kong Evangelical Church Chairman, Rev. Lo Bing Kuen, at Simon's memorial. He called it a "Letter Sent to Heaven":

> *I believe at this moment you have received the Lord's welcome and reward, and you are resting in Him. Although I truly believe this, it does not change the fact that we miss you or reduce our grief and sadness.*
>
> *I still remember one afternoon in July when I received a phone call at church. It was the first time I heard that you had an incurable disease. After hanging up, I sat on a bench in the sanctuary staring at the cross, which is located at the center of the stage. For a long time I could not say a word. The same question kept flashing through my mind: "Why*

you?" Someone has said, when calamity and sickness come people will ask three questions: (1) "Why me (or him)?" (2) "Why a Christian?" and (3) "Why a good Christian?"

As to your death, I want to add the word "young" to the third question; that is, "Why a young and good Christian?" Isn't it true? You were only 32 years old. You were younger than me. It was just a year ago that I congratulated you because you had finished your Master of Divinity degree and Clinical Pastoral Care in the hospital during your sabbatical year. Now is the time for you to work for God, but you are resting forever. How could you use what you had learned? I remember what the Bible says, "You don't even know what your life will be tomorrow! You are like a puff of smoke which appears for a moment and then disappears" (James 4:14).

You were not only young, you were also a good pastor. We had worked together for about ten years in the Hong Kong Evangelical Church. The impression you gave me was that you were very energetic, kind, friendly, and enthusiastic in spreading the Gospel. You had devoted your whole self to your "sheep." You were deeply loved by your co-workers and believers. Your death was surely a loss to our churches and the HKEC Conference. When you saw God, did you ask Him why He didn't cure you so you could keep serving Him and continue taking care of your wife and two boys?

Recently when I preached, I tried to use logic to help the congregation understand and accept that

God has good reasons to let suffering come to the ones that love Him. However, when I face your death I realize the answers I gave the congregation could not cast away my own doubts and perplexity. Even in suffering I believe God is still here and His love has not changed. I remember one true story. Near the end of World War II, the Allied Forces swept through Germany, searching every farmhouse for ambushers. In a deserted house the searchers with their flashlights went carefully down into the basement. A Star of David was found drawn on a collapsed wall. A few sentences were written below it. It was believed that they were written by a Jew before he was executed. The sentences are:

I believe there is a sun –
even when there is no sunshine;
I believe there is love –
even when love hasn't been shown;
I believe there is a God –
even if He doesn't speak.

How great are God's riches! How deep are His wisdom and knowledge! Who can explain His decisions? Who can understand His ways? As the scripture says, "Who knows the mind of the Lord? Who is able to give Him advice? Who has ever given Him anything, so that He had to pay it back? For all things were created by Him, and all things exist through Him and for Him. To God be the glory forever! Amen" (Romans 11:33-36).[34]

157

Rev. David and Cynthia Aufrance—on arrival both taught at United Christian College. David is OMS Field Leader, Chairman of the United Wesleyan Graduate Institute,, International Christian School Board Chairman, and Supervisor of UCC. Cindy is also very involved with each of the above.

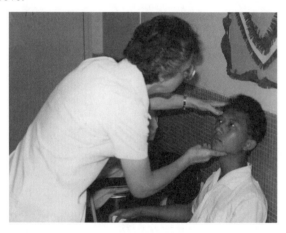

Dorothy checking Wing Tin's face after a fight with a classmate.

CHAPTER 22

MISSIONARY OUTREACH
OF THE HKEC & OMS HK

As you have read of the great heart and love of Rev. Simon Lee, an important event came out of the Yan Shek Church when Simon first became the senior pastor. A young seminary graduate, Miss Ruth Tang, had pastored at Yan Shek. During that time she sensed God's call on her life for full-time missionary service in another land. She applied to the Overseas Missionary Fellowship, (the former China Inland Mission) and was assigned to the Philippines, specifically to the Manila poor. It was a tough assignment, but she was willing to go. She also had to learn another language.

Ruth served in Manila and while there met a young American man, Mark McDowell, whose heart was burdened for the boys of the street and had a ministry with them. She and Mark fell in love and were married. They did their deputation in Hong Kong and also in the USA. Before they went back to the Philippines, a baby girl was born to them, whom they named Rainbow. Ruth was the first Chinese missionary to go from the HKEC churches, and since then several have gone to various parts in Asia.

MACAU--A JOINT MISSION WORK
WITH OMS AND HKEC

Macau, consisting of a tiny peninsula and two islands just 16 square kilometers in area, lies 40 miles west of Hong Kong on the coast of southern China. It was 1513 when the first Portuguese explorer arrived on the Pearl River Delta. About all that was there were two small temples dedicated to the goddess of the fishermen and the sea. From a small beginning Macau has developed a dismal inheritance. In the history of this piece of Chinese territory under Portuguese administration, every type of vice, corruption, idolatry, exploitation, and oppression usually associated with Asian and Western influence has existed and still abounds today. Gambling is Macau's major industry.[35]

The following paragraphs show how Field Director Dale McClain saw Macau in 1961, long before there was even a tiny crack in the Bamboo Curtain:

Macau is the oldest foreign settlement in the Far East. It has 140,000 residents. It is a refuge sought by those who would flee Red China. It was founded by Portugal's Leonel de Sousa just 65 years after Columbus' big incident in 1492. Blessed by the Chinese Emperor from his golden throne in Peking for their help in destroying the power of the pirating sea robbers, today it is a four and a half square-mile port on the edge of Red China.

Macau's 2,000 Protestant Christians look back, as does all Christendom, to the first herald of the Gospel to China—Robert Morrison. He is buried there. As we stood by his grave, we prayed earnestly in our hearts that God would raise up more Morrisons for our troubled world. Across the narrow waterway separating the tiny colony from China's Lappa Island can be seen the mouth of the West River arriving at its coastal destination. At its mouth a Communist forced-labor camp of 5,000 Chinese slaves are building a dam. The Communists call this dubious therapy "Labor Reform!" Most of the 5,000 are from the Central and Northern provinces.

Just 75 yards offshore stands Peking's alert marine sentinel—the Communist gunboat. Its job? To capture escapees or to machine gun those who get beyond their reach. In addition, they supervise the fishing catch of Macau's fishermen. Those who net in these waters must relinquish 50 percent of their fishing take to the Communist fisherman's commune across the way. That's the price of the entrance ticket to this fishing haven.

Walking through a Communist Chinese shop, the clerks treated me with coldness— if not hostility. At the Sing Kwong Communist Book Store, lovely classical music sounded forth from the latest Hi-Fi equipment. I bought three books including a large 56-page pictorial on Soviet Russia, a 30-page book on the subject, Chinese Women in the Great Leap Forward. The total price was US$0.60. In the above-mentioned book on the "Big Leap" (published 1960 by Peking Foreign Language Press), the propaganda quotes a lady character on page 25 as saying, "The coming of the Commune is

161

like getting to heaven in one jump." Our question is, "If this is the 'end' of the Big Leap, then why are so many running away?"[36]

From 1984-1987 the McClains returned to Hong Kong. Serving as field director again, Dale still carried a burden for Macau in his heart. Since the article above was written, much had changed in Macau. The Macau Bible Institute had been founded and the director was a friend of Dale's. Dale was asked to teach some Bible subjects at the institute, which he did with much joy. There was continued talk of having a mission church there in Macau, and Dale urged OMS and the HKEC to combine their resources to begin a new work.

Under Dale's leadership, OMS removed themselves from active participation of the Hong Kong Evangelical Church Executive Committee. We wanted the church to have more independence, especially as 1997 moved closer. This led to the forming of the Joint Committee where the OMS Field Committee sat with the leaders of the HKEC quarterly to discuss issues related to the ongoing work and developing a greater partnership.

In 1987-1988 Dr. and Mrs. Everett Hunt came to Hong Kong. Serving as interim field director, Ev taught at the Macau Bible Institute and encouraged the beginning of a Macau OMS-HKEC work. In 1988 the Macau Mission work, Dragon Garden Church, was started.

Macau returned to China sovereignty in December 1999, and now China has sovereignty over everything on the southern side of China except Taiwan.

DRAGON GARDEN CHURCH

On October 1, 1989, Rev. Tony Kwan and his wife, Portia, were called by God to come from Canada to serve at Dragon Garden Church in Macau. From there on, the church developed from a small group of students and Bible studies to an established church. They held regular Sunday school, prayer meetings, and fellowship meetings for children, high school students and adults as well as morning and evening worship services. Later, there were also care groups and a ministry committee established to make a better church.

Pastor Kwan, director of Development and HKEC Outreach Ministries, wrote the following:

> *Stanita Foundation, as a part of the Every Creature Crusade, initially sponsored a joint venture of OMS International and Hong Kong Evangelical Church, in which HKEC regarded the project as her first mission church outside of Hong Kong.*
>
> *Dragon Garden Church was established on March 28, 1988. The church is located at the intersection of Rua de Francis Xavier and Rua de Morais on the fifth floor of a high-rise building.*
>
> *The first full-time pastor/ECC team leader was Mrs. Chan Lui Sau-ling, wife of Rev. Chan Wing Fai, who was an experienced local pastor in Macau. Mr. Tam Shu Kong was sent by HKEC as a short-term mission worker in the church. He was a member of Yan Yue Church. To begin with, the church also provided study help for the local*

163

students. *Because of that, a number of students were reached for Christ. In May 1988, Rev. and Mrs. Chan left the church for further theological training in Canada.*

During this time, some of the coworkers from HKEC went to Macau on a part-time basis to help out. These workers included Ms. Chow Ka Chun and Mr. Tang Shun Chuen. In November Mrs. Chui, a local Bible woman, was recruited to serve the church as a part-time worker until the end of April 1993.

From 1990 until now, each year there has been at least one short-term mission group coming from Hong Kong or elsewhere to work on evangelistic mission teams for the church. This has become a popular spot for short-term missions. Over these years, hundreds of people made decisions to follow Christ. Some of these people came from China mainland, as contract workers. They are contracted for two years and are told not to get involved with any religious groups. The hours they work may be 12 or more in a day, so it is hard to find a time when these busy immigrants are free to talk. Some come and hear the Word about Jesus' love and believe. Then they take the Gospel of Christ back to China.

The first baptismal service was held on Easter Sunday of 1990 and four were baptized by Rev. Gerud Helsby, then Field Director of OMS Hong Kong. We had the second baptismal service with Rev. Dale McClain as the honorable guest speaker.

From 1990 there were baptismal services each year, and in 1992 the church built its own baptismal pool.

In September 1992, Stella Chu Ying-Yee joined the church as a full-time evangelist. She had just graduated from the Macau Bible Institute. Stella had her internship in the church in the two years before graduation. The Lord prepared her to be the pastor of the church when in October 1994 I was transferred back to Hong Kong to be the director of Development of the Hong Kong Evangelical Church.

The Dragon Garden Church is not yet self-supporting, and they are receiving funds from the HKEC Mission Fund. Their goal is to be self-supporting by 2003. Stella Chu has been working hard toward this target date. There needs to be more whole families coming to know the Lord and be involved in the church. Macau is a hard mission field and more workers are needed.

DAVID LONG FAMILY ARRIVES

In September 1995 OMS missionaries David and Lori Long arrived with their three children, Benjamin, Anna, and Abby. They moved to Macau to study and be more immersed in the Cantonese language. On weekends they served in the church. Dragon Garden Church sponsored the Longs in order for them to get their work permit and residence status there in Macau. God worked things out in His plan. The church works hand-in-hand with OMS to expand His Kingdom on earth.

The last year of the Longs' first term was spent living in southern China. This experience gave them more opportunity to hear only the Cantonese language and to make some wonderful friends. Through some conversational English classes, they were able to share about their Savior as the situations arose. Dr. Helen Lewis, who had spent some years teaching in Hong Kong in the '80s, although now retired, went to China for the year to teach the children, Benjamin, Anna, and Abby.

David was a practicing lawyer in Kentucky until he felt God's call to missions. He then went to Asbury Seminary in Wilmore, Kentucky. What a wonderful answer to prayer when God led them to Hong Kong. They are back in Hong Kong after their study furlough. David has been involved with discipleship and training and with the beginning of the United Wesleyan Graduate Institute. He also serves as the field treasurer. Benjamin, Anna, and Abby attend the International Christian School that OMS helped found.

The David Long family in 1996.

Our mission field within a mission field: Evie—Chinese American Christian, Divya—a Hindu from India, Susan—a Christian; the boys in the back: Ivan—a Hindu from India, Kenny—a missionary kid, a Chinese who doesn't claim anything.

Dr. Paul Hau-lim Pang turned the Principalship over to Dr. David Chi Shang To.

Dr. Pang became President of the Research Institute for Christian Education—Left to Right, Dr. Paul Pang, Dr. Ed Erny—Interim Field Leader, some teachers from China and Dorothy Backer.

Dr. David Chi Shang To cutting the ribbon to open the Exhibition.

CHAPTER 23

CHINA MINISTRIES FROM HONG KONG

HONG KONG EVANGELICAL CHURCH
(HKEC)

Rev. Tony Kwan, HKEC Director of Development and Missions Outreach, wrote the following:

A few years before 1997, HKEC had explored the possibilities of serving the people in the mainland. The younger generation has the zeal to minister to the Chinese in the mainland. Some short-term missions and ministry projects helped the Chinese Christians and local people through charitable work, nurture of believers, caring ministry, and sharing the Word of God. There was good response from the mainlanders. However, due to the change of status of Hong Kong to become a Special Administrative Region of China after July 1, 1997, HKEC needs to serve China as a whole in a wise way.

Many of our co-workers in HKEC have been very careful to do their works quietly without fanfare or advertisement, especially as related to China. They do not share names, deeds, or places

169

except to those who need to know. Perhaps their fears are not unfounded since they know how the authorities across the border in China could make a case for their arrest over some small thing. Many Christians in China have been arrested for meeting in unregistered places to worship God and read His Word if they have it. Even with some areas more open and also being able to have Bibles printed in China, all of China does not enjoy religious freedom. We are thankful for our brothers and sisters who do have some ministry in south China and we pray for a more open door for the sake of the Gospel.

STREAMS IN THE DESERT

A ministry that OMS has been involved in for many years (although not as a "hands on" ministry) is one that isn't talked about much. That is the broadcasting of *Streams in the Desert* into Mainland China.

What is *Streams in the Desert*? This devotional book, on which the radio program is based, was written over a period of about six years. The author, Lettie Cowman, wife of the founder of The Oriental Missionary Society, wrote about her struggles and the lessons God taught her during the period when her husband, Charles Cowman, lay sick and at times near death. She learned many lessons in this difficult time about a God who loved and cared for her even in hardships. Because she wrote these lessons down, many people have benefited. China's Christians relate very well to Lettie Cowman's struggles because difficulties for a Christian in China is a way of life. As a result, *Streams in the Desert* is the most popular Christian book in China only after the Bible.

Grant Nealis recalls that the first tapes were made in Taiwan and were broadcast over Far Eastern Broadcasting Company (FEBC) and Trans World Radio (TWR) via shortwave. Asian Outreach, a sister mission in Hong Kong, had various ministries in China. David Wang, International Director of Asian Outreach (AO), after his first trip back into China for some years, spoke to Grant about the *Streams* broadcast. He felt that the announcers' Taiwan-spoken Mandarin was too noticeable and Taiwanese broadcasters weren't acquainted enough with the situation in China to make the material meaningful for the Mainlanders. (In those days the Taiwan people were not allowed into the Mainland.)

David Wang approached OMS about letting Asian Outreach prepare the recordings in their Hong Kong studios. Asian Outreach would cover the costs of preparation and OMS, the costs of airtime. We had already been working with AO in printing copies of *Streams in the Desert* in Japan and Hong Kong by the 10,000 lot for distribution in China. AO did most of the distributing, but OMS had copies as well for their own distribution. This was in 1978-79 after former President Richard Nixon's trip to Beijing.

A contract was signed between the parties involved—OMS, AO, FEBC, and TWR—beginning a broadcasting partnership on short wave with both FEBC and TWR. As OMS' finances for this project began to diminish, we had to make a decision based on listener response. At their own expense, FEBC had begun re-broadcasting the tapes on their new standard band station in Korea. They were receiving more letter responses from this broadcast than from either of the shortwave broadcasts. Because of financial concerns, we began paying for airtime on FEBC's standard broadcast.

The first broadcasts must have started sometime in the mid-'70s. Grant Nealis recalls that when he and his son, Jon, made their first trip to China in 1978, TWR asked them to take shortwave radios with them and check the quality of the broadcasts.

The partnership between OMS, AO, and FEBC lasted about 20 years. As changes have come to Hong Kong and China, OMS has tried to keep the *Streams* program financed and on the air into China. The rising costs of production and airtime have necessitated that OMS cut back on the radio project. Funds now go into other China ministries.

Asian Outreach continued to help OMS print *Streams in the Desert* in the Mainland Chinese script. While Harry Lee was living, he spoke in many places in the United States and Canada and helped fund these projects. His story, *From the Claws of the Dragon*, tells of God's faithfulness through his years in China and in prison for his faith. Harry died in April, 1996 from a fast-growing brain tumor and is greatly missed by many.

Why do the Chinese in China love Mrs. Cowman's *Streams* so much? David Wang says,

> *In the interior of China, the* Streams *in the* Desert *devotional has become synonymous with religious broadcasting in general. Mrs. Cowman has done an excellent job of using the elements of nature such as the mountains, rivers, wind, and*

animals to create word pictures that Chinese people identify with and understand. When you add those to her message of God's faithfulness in times of suffering and persecution, it speaks to the heart of the whole nation.

In a letter to Dale McClain in February 1987, David wrote the following:

Last week some of our co-workers went into China and had a day of fellowship with several pastors from a distant province. As you know, God's spirit is really moving in that particular province and many people are coming to Christ. Streams in the Desert *is still the number two item wanted by the Christians in China besides the Bible...*

When I was in Inner Mongolia, I was introduced to a Christian family. I asked the family if they were listening to Gospel broadcasts. The lady told me that they listen to Streams in the Desert *all the time. At another place a Christian lady in an open Three-Self Church approached one of our staff. The lady asked if they had any Christian literature for them such as* Streams in the Desert*?*

...One of my co-workers just returned from meeting an elderly pastor in Central China. This pastor who is in his sixties has to oversee 138 meeting points. He shared with us that there are still many Christians in these areas who do not have a Bible nor any literature at all. Our co-workers brought him four bags of Bibles, Streams

in the Desert, *and other literature. While they were talking with him, a group of Christians from some other villages came to visit. The moment they saw the four bags of literature, they grabbed the bags and begged the pastor to let them bring the literature back to their churches. Such is the need for Christian literature in China.*

LETTERS FROM LISTENERS IN CHINA

The following letters are history, but they reflect the hearts of disillusioned youth of the times. These two letters were received in August 1989, just two months after the student uprising and massacre in Tiananmen Square on June 4, 1989.

Testimony #1

I am a university student. Some time ago, I was challenged by the Students' Movement in Beijing. I wanted to join them to fight for China, to topple the corrupted government, and to regain freedom for China. However, I was totally disappointed.

After some time, I accidentally came across your program. Suddenly I realized that only the Lord Jesus can save our suffering nation. In the past, I was blind and lacked faith. I was fighting for an "ideal" then. But now I realized that the Lord is more important than ideals.

Your Streams in the Desert *program is really like a stream that satisfies my longing soul. I believe in what the Lord said: "To know the Truth*

174

is to have life." However, my knowledge of God is only limited to the radio broadcasts. Please help me to become a part of the family of God. What should I do now? How can I really serve the Lord and be a true Christian? How can I receive forgiveness from Christ?

<u>Testimony #2</u>

I am a university lecturer. I was very concerned for the Students' Movement and monitored the development closely. I started listening to your programs during the Students' Movement and felt that they were really relevant to China. Please send me a Bible. And please let me know how I can qualify to become a Christian and a worshiper of God.

HKEC was challenged to help support the *Streams* broadcast. A majority of the churches responded and in one more way, the Hong Kong Christians are becoming involved in tangible ways with their brothers and sisters in China. More individuals are sharing Jesus with their relatives and friends, as they are able.

175

Crusader Billy Campbell teaching a song to some villagers in the "Closed Area" – between Hong Kong and China.

Rev. Billy and Jeanne Campbell and their two daughters, Kathleen and Caroline.

CHAPTER 24

MAJOR EVENTS IN HONG KONG

An event occurring in December 1984 again changed the course of Hong Kong.

On December 19, 1984, the Prime Minister of the United Kingdom of Great Britain and Northern Ireland, Mrs. Margaret Thatcher, and the Prime Minister of the People's Republic of China, Mr. Zhao Ziyang, acting on behalf of their respective governments, signed the following agreement on the future of Hong Kong:

JOINT DECLARATION OF THE GOVERNMENT OF THE UNITED KINGDOM OF GREAT BRITAIN AND NORTHERN IRELAND AND THE GOVERNMENT OF THE PEOPLE'S REPUBLIC OF CHINA ON THE QUESTION OF HONG KONG

The government of the United Kingdom of Great Britain and Northern Ireland and the government of the People's Republic of China have reviewed with satisfaction the friendly relations existing between the two governments and peoples in recent years and agreed that a proper negotiated settlement of the question of Hong Kong, which is left over from the past, is

177

conducive to the maintenance of the prosperity and stability of Hong Kong.

1. The government of the People's Republic of China declares that to recover the Hong Kong area is the common aspiration of the entire Chinese people, and that it has decided to resume the exercise of sovereignty over Hong Kong with effect from July 1, 1997.

2. The Government of the United Kingdom declares that it will restore Hong Kong to the People's Republic of China with effect from July 1, 1997.

3. The People's Republic of China has decided to establish a Hong Kong Special Administrative Region upon resuming the exercise of sovereignty over Hong Kong.[37]

Up to 31 pages of notes related to the handover of Hong Kong are couched in nebulous jargon. It is now an accomplished fact and Hong Kong is again part of China. China is rewriting the history books to make them look good but is leaving out much of the history that really made Hong Kong what it is today.

Britain had ruled over the colony for more than 150 years. Much of Hong Kong was leased in 1898 from China for 99 years. Although the people of Hong Kong were mixed in their opinions as to whether they wanted Great Britain to continue as landlords or to return to China, the handover was a "done deal." China promised to allow Hong Kong to maintain its capitalistic system for another 50 years.

One thing the evangelical churches feared was that the China Religious Bureau would want to bring the Hong Kong churches under its domain. Thank the Lord that they have not done that.

On the other hand, they have not allowed the Hong Kong churches to be actively involved with Christian work in China. Times of uncertainty often bring us closer to God, and that has been true of Hong Kong people and many of the churches.

The pastors began to emphasize more training of lay people to be able to teach and lead small cell groups in individual homes. My pastor, Rev. Lee, grouped the congregation according to the districts in which they lived. A leader was chosen for each division. When the small groups met, Pastor Simon took turns meeting with them to help in training and guidance. He wanted his people to be better equipped and to know the Word of God to enable them to stand firm in their faith, even through the worst scenario.

It was a wonderful thing to see the courage and move-ahead attitude of many of our pastors and workers. What one pastor said in a sermon is a challenge no matter when it was said. "Do not worry about the years to come. Consider your relationship to Christ today. What are you doing to expand His kingdom?"

What happened on July 1, 1997, is history, but the whole world was watching. On this day of pomp and splendor, with British Royalty and many high-ranking officials present, thousands of Hong Kong rank and file everywhere vied for a glimpse of important personages. That day Chinese President Jiang Zemin was the first head of state from the mainland to set foot in Hong Kong in all its years as a colony. Earlier ceremonies included a parade and the traditional British farewell during which the Royal Marines Band played in a typical Hong Kong summer downpour. Prince Charles got soaked giving his farewell speech even with a large umbrella over him. The Union Jack came down its pole seconds before midnight and the "Five-star Red Flag" reached the top of its staff eight seconds after the hour.

China's plan of sending 4,000 troops over the border into Hong Kong just a few hours after the take-over caused some concern. They came by transport trucks, ships, and helicopters. The new Hong Kong CEO, Tung Chee-hwa, called the troops a necessary symbol of Beijing's sovereignty.

The new Beijing-backed chief executive said a few days after the handover that the people in this prosperous new Chinese territory will have to learn the ways of their ancient motherland if they are to be trusted. This man has been bowing to Beijing ever since , which is not always in favor of the needs of the Hong Kong people. Pro-democracy people have been neatly excluded from the governing body, and anything considered anti-China is squelched. One example of this is the canceling of continuing celebrations of remembering the young who died at the Tienanmen Square protest on June 4, 1989.[38]

"ONE COUNTRY, TWO SYSTEMS"

The ingenious and novel concept of "one country, two systems," which was first put forward by Mr. Deng Xiaoping (late China Premier) in the late 1970s, laid the solid foundation for the eventual reunification of the country. It was decided that upon China's resumption of the exercise of sovereignty over Hong Kong, a Hong Kong Special Administrative Region would be established in accordance with the provisions of Article 31 of the Constitution of the People's Republic of China, and that under the principle of "one country, two systems," the socialist system and policies would not be practiced in Hong Kong.[39]

Hong Kong underwent a constitutional change on July 1, 1997, when it became a Special Administrative Region of the People's Republic of China. Following the end of British administration at midnight on June 30, 1997, the Basic Law, which is the constitutional document of the Hong Kong SAR, came into effect. The Basic Law sets out in a legal document the Chinese Government's basic policies towards Hong Kong and the way in which the HKSAR is to be administered for 50 years beyond 1997. Under the Basic Law, the HKSAR shall enjoy a high degree of autonomy except in defense and foreign affairs.[40]

These details enable us to compare current events in Hong Kong with the promises given in 1997. Already issues have been clouding the horizon and people wonder where the Basic Law policies went.

The Hong Kong Court of Final Appeals, like the United States Supreme Court, made a ruling on a large group of people who had overstayed their time in Hong Kong. The Hong Kong CEO did not like the court's ruling and appealed to the Standing Committee of the National People's Congress in Beijing to reinterpret that law. Many people saw this as a serious breech of China's pledge to allow "Hong Kong people to rule Hong Kong" for the next 50 years.[41]

Following are two comments taken from Hong Kong newspapers that show concerns in Hong Kong:

The Chief Executive or anyone inside or outside of the Government could theoretically go to China to reinterpret any ruling made by a Hong Kong court if they did not agree with that decision.

The Court of Final Appeal has no real power to decide anything lasting that cannot be overturned by China. It is at the mercy of whichever way the political winds are blowing in China.

Isn't it a comfort and strength to know that what our God promises, He brings to pass. In Him is stability and security. He is our refuge and strength; He is our strong tower; He is!

On a victorious note, think about the fact that for years OMS tried to restart a seminary in Hong Kong and nothing seemed to come together. Now even with the change in government in Hong Kong, a seminary is beginning. People are in place as professors and administrators, and some are preparing to go to Hong Kong for the seminary and training ministry. To God be the Glory. His church will stand, no matter what or where!

Finally, be strong in the Lord and in His mighty power. Put on the full armor of God so you can take your stand against the devil and his schemes. For our struggle is not against flesh and blood, but against the rulers, against the authorities, against the powers of this dark world and against the spiritual forces of evil in the heavenly realms (Ephesians 6:10-12).

Right at the back of the church—really a postage stamp size of ground.

Rev. Simon Lee, his wife, Miu Sheung, and little boy Hin Ching.

It is Chinese New Year in the home of Rev. and Mrs. Micah Tong. Micah pastored one of the HKEC churches as well as serving as Chair-Man of the HKEC Conference. Claudia is the Conference General Secretary.

Pastors and co-workers gathered for their prayer and business meeting. This time they farewell Dorothy Backer.

Gloria Kong—Chinese secretary, bookkeeper, and a wonderful
Christian friend, the one who keeps the Field Leader on track.

Rev. Dale and Polly McClain went back to Hong Kong mid 80's
to serve another term. God took Dale to heaven before all his
stories could be written down.

Bill and Becky Swathwood, presently in charge of the English Ministry in Hong Kong.

Rev. David and Cynthia Aufrance—present Field Leaders.

Taylor and Mari Hubbard and children – Taylor taught at United Christian College until the government made all schools teach in the Chinese language. Now Taylor teaches at the International Christian School.

Rev. Mel Kizer returned to Hong Kong to supervise the building project.

Seminary students and teaching staff.

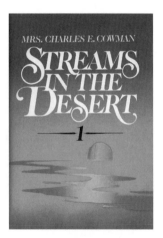

"Streams," is a much loved devotional book by Mrs. Charles Cowman.

CHAPTER 25

CHARTS AND THINGS

STAGE DURATION	PERIODS	CHARACTERISTICS
First Stage 1954-1960	Planting churches through education	Churches established through education directly belonged to Oriental Missionary Society. Two churches begun through rooftop schools: Ling Yan and Chuk Yuen. Three more churches were established in this period: Grace Church, Yan Yue, and Yan Chiu.
Second Stage 1961-1973	Planting churches through door-to-door evangelism in rural areas	Every Creature Crusade (ECC) ministry started to work in the New Territories. Church planting worked through door-to-door evangelism. Planted churches directly belonged to the Oriental Missionary Society. Church established in this period were: Yan Din, Yan Chaak, Yan Shek, Yan Yau Church. Up to 1973, HKEC had seven local churches.

Third Stage 1974 to mid-1991	Planting churches through social services	We applied to the Hong Kong Government to operate social services centers in the name of "Hong Kong Evangelical Church" and we used the government facilities for social service and planting churches. Churches planted in this period were Yan Kei, Yan Ying, Yan Fook, Yan Tsuen, and Yan Lam Church. (We also had a mission field in Macau Dragon Garden Church.) Up to mid-1991 HKEC had 13 churches.

OMS Hong Kong Field Directors
1953-2000

Highlights during each one's ministry

1953-1958	Rev. Harry Woods and Mrs. Florence Munroe.	The Hong Kong work was established, offices set up, two churches started, three rooftop schools registered, a former student from OMS Canton seminary came to help, many baptized and brought into the church and teachers found for the rooftop schools.
1958-1965	Rev. Dale McClain	The OMS Seminary began; the teachers wanting to know more about the Bible were the early students. The Every Creature Crusade was started in Hong Kong. The vision to have our own center in Kowloon was born and Dale saw the Chung Yan Primary School and the Kau Yan Medical Center built and opened. Work on the church had begun before Dale and Polly left for the USA in 1965.Three churches started, two through the ECC teams.

1965-1971	Rev. Robert Erny	The seminary was discontinued because of lack of students. Grace Rock Church was built and the old Yan Kwong and the small Tai Po Street Church joined and moved into the new church structure. The clinic closed in 1970 because of no doctor and spiraling medical costs. The large Wong Tai Sin Rooftop school established a church held on the rooftop. The ECC TEAM began the Chuen Wan Chapel.
1971-1984	Rev. Grant Nealis (Nealis furlough) Rev. E. H. (Buddy) Gaines III Rev. Melvin Kizer	Grant worked with the ECC team in Chuen Wan and it was this chapel that became the Bryan Memorial, in honor of Dorothy Bryan Nealis' parents. Grant helped the Hong Kong Evangelical Church Conference to begin purchasing apartments to use as meeting halls. The Revolving Loan Fund was set up to help with this need. The biggest highlight during Grant's tenure was the birth of the idea for the high school. Along with Dr. Paul Pang, they dreamed of establishing United Christian College. It came true in 1974 and hundreds of young people have come to know the Lord in these past 25 years.

1970's	Rev. Grant Nealis	The creative idea of applying to the government for reading centers in the new housing estates was born and OMS obtained three reading study centers and one social service center for the elderly. Churches were begun through each of these centers. A youth ministry department was set up under Grant with Buddy Gaines as the director. In 1975, the Rose Court apartments on Rose Street were purchased for missionary housing, the first property bought by OMS HK.
1984-1987	Rev. Dale Mc-Clain	Dale and Polly McClain returned to HK to give leadership after the Nealis family left for the USA. During this time, the preliminary planning took place for the new Christian Education Building, and the blueprints were drawn. This building was built behind Grace Church, next to the mountain. OMS purchased another apartment for missionaries – Joy Garden, Alnwick Road, Beacon Hill, Kowloon. Dale spent time in Macau teaching at the Macau Bible Institute and had a growing burden for OMS to have a church there. OMS removed themselves from active participation on the Hong Kong Evangelical Church Executive Committee. OMS wanted the church to have more independence, especially as 1997 moved closer. This led to the forming of the Joint Committee where the OMS Field Committee sat with the leaders of the HKEC to discuss issues related to the ongoing work and developing a greater partnership.

1987-1988	Dr. Everett N. Hunt	Ev and Carroll Hunt came as Interim Director so Gerud Helsby could continue language school before becoming Field Director. Ev taught at the Macau Bible Institute and continued encouraging HKEC to join with OMS in starting a work in Macau. The Macau mission work began in 1988. Ev and Carroll returned to Kentucky to teach in Asbury Seminary. Gery Helsby became Field Director.
1988-1991	Rev. Gerud Helsby	The first family service center opened in Sheung Shui in the Choi Yuen Housing Estate. Rev. Sunny Chow led the way in this first of a kind evangelistic opportunity. Ministering to the whole family. During this period of time the Stanita Foundation cut their amount of financial support for the ECC ministry. This required that our ECC program and the HKEC begin making a plan to be entirely self-supporting. The new Christian Educational Building went up and the OMS offices were moved onto the ninth floor. Gery was one of the men with a vision for a Christian High School. OMS and several other mission groups brought the International Christian School into being, which now has around 400 students. Not only are there missionary kids in the student body but also other nationalities who speak English and need the American school system. This mix of young people gives great opportunity for evangelism. OMS purchased more missionary housing in Sai Kung in the New Territories. Gery was asked to return to OMS headquarters to become Vice-President of Homeland Ministries.

| 1991 - 2000 | Rev. David Aufrance, furlough

Dr. Ed Erny – Interim Director- 1995-96 | Dave continued on the Board of Directors at the International Christian School (ICS). Since OMS was one of the founding missions, several of our missionaries have continued to help at the Board level. Dave was also the Supervisor of United Christian College and served on the Board of Directors and Managers. He taught at UCC for many years. The HKEC moved right ahead and several of our well-established churches planted daughter churches.

When OMS moved out of the offices in Grace Church and Grace Church took over the whole building, the need arose for the lease agreement to be renegotiated. The reason for this was that the land belonged to OMS and not the church. This created some difficulties because the other churches purchased their meeting halls. This agreement had been drawn up ten years previously between Grace Church, UCC, and OMS, regarding paying rent for use of the facility and responsibility for repairs, etc. The rent monies went into the Church Revolving Loan Fund, the Repair Fund, and HKEC. Negotiations were not easy, but God moved in hearts and the new agreement was finished in 1999. The 1997 Handover of Hong Kong by Britain to China sovereignty was a history making year. |

OMS HONG KONG MISSIONARIES

NAME	YEARS OF SERVICE
Mrs. Florence Munroe	1953-1964
Rev. Lee and Helen Hobel	1955-1959
Rev. Dale and Pauline McClain	1957-1965
	1984-1987
Miss Mary Ellen Beetley	1958-1987
Rev. Robert and Phyllis Erny	1959-1971
Mr. Edgar H. Gaines III (Buddy)-Crusader	1960-1964
Mr. Charles McNelly –Crusader	1960-1963
Rev. Grant and Dorothy Nealis	1961-1984
Mr. Ron and Priscilla Harrington	1962-1966
Mr. Duane Beals--Crusader	1963-1965
Miss Dorothy Backer	1963-1996
Dr. Charles and Joanne Omdal	1965-1970
Mr. Billy Campbell—Crusader	1965-1968
Miss Marilyn Snider	1966-2000+
Mr. Bob Hale—Crusader	1968-1971
Rev. Buddy and Marti Gaines	1969-1978
Miss Joyce Barber	1972-1973
Miss Effie Tucker	1973-
Rev. Billy and Jeanne Campbell	1970-1975 and 1996
Rev. Melvin and Nancy Kizer	1974-1983
Rev. Mel Kizer	1987-1989
Mr. David and Cynthia Aufrance+	1975-2000+

Mr. Roger and Jeanette Davis	1978-1980
Dr. P. Helen Lewis	1980-1982
	1998-1999
Miss Sally Overton	1985-1987
Mr. James and Nell Oldham	1986-1987
Rev. Gerud and Anne Helsby	1986-1991
Dr. Everett and Carroll Hunt	1987-1988
Miss Kathleen Campbell	1990-1991
Rev. David and Rozanne Rucker	1990-1993
Miss Karla Haden	1990-1996
Miss Colleen Taylor	1990-1991
Ms. Susan Dean	1991-1993
Miss Judith Cunningham	1991-1992
Mr. Mike Couvion	1992-1994
Miss Bethany Shull	1992-1994
Miss Kathy Fouts	1993-1994
Ms. Laurie Ferguson	1993-1995
Mr. David Gilham	1993-1995
Mr. Bill and Becky Swathwood	1994-2000+
Mr. David and Lori Long	1995-2000+
Dr. Edward and Rachel Erny	1995-1996
Miss Heidi Lawson	1996-1997
Miss LeAnn Seward	1996-1997
Mr. Howard and Joyce Cogswell	1996-1997
Mr. Taylor and Mari Hubbard	1996-2000+
Miss Hazel Williams	1999-2000

+Denotes active service

NOTES

OMS AT A GLANCE

The year was 1900. At a desk in Chicago's central Western Union office sat Charles Cowman, a young executive responsible for the supervision of 500 telegraph operators. He was hardly conscious of the incessant chatter of telegraph keys tapping out messages from every point on the globe. His mind was now occupied with another message – the call of Jesus to go into all the world with the good news.

Today, OMS International, the agency born of Cowman's response, is sending teams to the former Soviet Union, Eastern Europe, the Middle East, Asia, Africa, South America, Haiti and other nations.

OMS has no church denomination underwriting its work. Each of more than 450 missionaries trusts God to provide his support through the prayers and gifts of His people.

OMS exists to promote missionary outreach by mobilizing prayer, people, and financial resources for evangelism, church planting and leadership training. Our purpose is to: (1) engage in culturally relevant evangelism; (2) establish organizationally autonomous, culturally indigenous and spiritually reproductive churches; (3) train servant leaders to reach their nations; and (4) partner with them to reach the world for Christ.

OMS works in partnership with over 7,800 national workers and 5,242 organized churches whose membership exceeds one million. In 31 seminaries and 6,822 institutions, 6,822 students are preparing for ministry. Through door-to-door evangelism, 346 teams lead thousands to Christ and assist in establishing over four new congregations weekly. OMS outreach includes eight radio stations and ten medical clinics.

For information write OMS International, Box A, Greenwood, Indiana 46142-6599, or call 317/881-6751.

Upon a gift of $10 or support in a missionary, a quarterly publication, *OMS Outreach*, will be sent.

1. Endacott, G. B.: *A History of HONG KONG,* Oxford University Press, 1973, p.1

2. Endacott, G. B.: op. cit. pp 16-18

3. Broomhall, A. J.: *HUDSON TAYLOR 7 CHINA'S OPEN CENTURY,* Book One, *Barbarians at the Gates,* Hodder and Stoughton and The Overseas Missionary Fellowship, 1981, pp 267-268

4. Munroe, Mrs. Florence: *Harbor of Hope,* The Oriental Missionary Society, 1963 p. 19

5. Munroe, Mrs. Florence: Taken from many of her prayer letters and early Missionary Standard articles.

6. Munroe, Mrs. Florence: *Harbor of Hope*, The Oriental Missionary Society, 1963 p. 19

7. Helsby, Anne: Preparing to Stay, OMS OUT-REACH, November/December 1989 pp 19-21

8. Munroe, Mrs. Florence: *Harbor of Hope,* The Oriental Missionary Society, 1963 p. 13

9. Munroe, Mrs. Florence: Ibid, pp 18-19

10. Munroe, Mrs. Florence: Ibid, pp 21-23

11.   Munroe, Mrs. Florence: From one of her many early prayer letters, 1955-56

12.   Munroe, Mrs. Florence: "Rector on a Rooftop," *The Missionary Standard*, May, 1965 p 10-11

13.   Notes about Mr. And Mrs. Lee Chi Yiu were taken from early co-workers reports and prayer letters.

14.   Hong Kong Archives: 1963 Field Director's Report - Dale McClain

15.   Hong Kong Archives: From an article written by Mrs. Florence Munroe about 1979

16.   Ibid.
17.   Translated from the 10th Anniversary (1954-1964) booklet of OMS in Hong Kong.

18.   Nealis, Grant: Taken from a letter written by the Nealis' to raise money for the chapel

19.   Aufrance, Cynthia: "From HEROIN to HOPE and Life," *OMS Outreach*, Oct/Dec.1994

20.   Backer, Dorothy: "Tokens of Forgiveness," *OMS Outreach*, March 1975

21.   Notes taken from an interview with Holly Leung, March 1999

22. Notes from Rev. Billy Campbell's letter to Dorothy Backer, 1998

23. Campbell, Rev. Billy, from an article on Evangelism and Church Planting, 1996

24. Ibid:

25. Ibid:

26. "Frontlines," *The Missionary Standard*, December, 1972

27. Campbell, Jeanne: "It Happened One Saturday," *The Missionary Standard*, February, 1972

28. Nealis, Grant: "How God Builds A Church," *OMS Outreach*, April 1974

29. United Christian College, 20th Anniversary Book 1974-1994 "In Focus. . ."

30. Snider, Marilyn: "IN HONG KONG Pointing the Way to the Shepherd," *OMS Outreach*/No.4-1976 p.3-4

31. Backer, Dorothy: "Band Aids and Prepositions," *OMS Outreach*, Vol.27, No.7/1986

32. Aufrance, Cindy: "A Refuge For A Hoary Head," *OMS Outreach*/No. 3-1983

33. Chow, Sonny Ka Shing: "Through Death's Dark Vale," *OMS Outreach*, 1990

34. Loh, Terrance Bing Kuen: "A Letter Sent to Heaven," taken from a memorial booklet put together by the people of Zion Church, called *A Heart for God - Rev. Simon Lee.*

35. Asian Outreach in Macau pamphlet: Hong Kong, March 1995

36. McClain, Dale: "Dateline: MACAU," *The Missionary Standard*, February, 1961 p 5

37. HONG KONG 1985 - A REVIEW OF 1984: H. Myers, Government Printer at the Government Printing Department, Hong Kong. pp. 1-3 on up to p.31

38. Notations of the 1997 handover ceremony taken from various newspaper clippings from June 30-July 1, 1997.

39. *HONG KONG ••A NEW ERA•• A REVIEW OF 1997*: Editor-Bob Howlett; HK Government Information Services; Hong Kong Government Publications. Pp 5.

40. Ibid. p. 12.

41. Notes from David Aufrance's "Monday Fodder," December 10, 1999. Hong Kong Field Director.